AWAKENING ON PURPOSE

TRUSTING THE CALL

STEPHANIE HREHIRCHUK

Edited by
MARAYA LOZA KOXAHN

Editor: Maraya Loza-Koxahn

Cover Design: Rachel Betters

ISBN : 978-1-9991300-2-2

ISBN 978-1-9991300-3-9 (ebook)

For my teachers

CONTENTS

PROLOGUE

THE STUFF OF LEGENDS

"I see you writing." Sophie's hands glided through the air above me as I lay on her reiki table.

"Yes, I am writing. So much has opened up during my year in yoga. I can't stop writing." I smiled, pleased with Sophie's confirmation of what I deemed my newfound direction in life.

"I see you writing... the children's books," Sophie's native French revealed itself in her word choice. "You write the children's books."

My smile broke. "No, not children's books. They're not even on my radar."

"Hmmm, well, these things are like bubbles floating around you. All possibilities. You choose which ones." Sophie moved her hands toward my feet, and I knew the session was nearly done. Grounding through my feet always completed our time together. But I could tell by the look on Sophie's face, she didn't believe that the children's book bubble was only one of many possibilities.

"And now with your year in yoga finished, what will you

do? Your back is good, no?" She handed me a glass of water as I sat up on her treatment table.

"Yes, my back is amazing." I sipped the water, happy to continue our conversation. I loved her reiki room: essential oils and angelic music sweetened the air while Sophie's warm, welcoming nature soothed my soul. She was equal parts therapist and friend. "This past year in yoga inquiries, moving through a chakra every forty days at the cabin outside Bragg Creek, was one of the most challenging yet transformative periods of my life. I woke up, Sophie... to something bigger than me, but still me. There is so much aliveness around us. Angels, aliens, deities... I don't know... but I do know I'm not going back to sleep. My spine healed, yes, and there is more harmony in my home and my family."

"Yes, this is good. I can see it with you and your children. But there's something else." Sophie knew me well.

"I don't know. It should all be enough... this incredible gift of awakening should be enough."

"But..."

"I feel unsettled." I slid off the edge of her table and into my shoes. "Well, not quite unsettled, more like... driven. Like there's something more I'm meant to be doing. There's got to be a reason I woke up. There must be a greater purpose to my life."

"I see," she handed me my phone. "These things tend to reveal themselves in their own time."

"I guess." I hugged Sophie. "For now, I'm grateful for everything in my life... including you, my friend." I sauntered along the path between her home and mine, looking out at the Rocky Mountains. *I hope my purpose reveals itself. Because I don't know which is worse: not waking up or never realizing what you woke up to do.*

I thought I had it all figured out, or, at least, I figured I was content with what I had: the return of my health, invigoration for life, appreciation for family and friends, a rich inner life. But Spirit wasn't done with me. I had merely stepped out of yoga school and into nature school. It would require all of my tools from the previous year to see me through the forthcoming lessons. The most important tool: trust.

In Paulo Coehlo's *The Alchemist*, he writes of the *Personal Legend*: what his main character came to do in his lifetime. Life purpose, let's say. Before my spiritual awakening, I thought little of it, only what I wanted to do for work or entertainment or health. But my year in yoga had awakened me and, the sleeping giant, my Personal Legend. It had begun to scratch at the seams of my mind. And, like Coehlo's main character, I would only know it through the language of nature: a language I had yet to learn or had long forgotten.

"To romanticize the world is to make us aware of the magic, mystery and wonder of the world; it is to educate the senses to see the ordinary as extraordinary, the familiar as strange, the mundane as sacred, the finite as infinite."

— NOVALIS

PART I

SUMMER SCHOOL

1

INITIATION

I saw the women. They brushed each other's hair, adorning one another with flowers. I saw the men, below by the pond. The hilltop hosted a ceremonial site, not for dancing and music but for women's ritual, perhaps a rite of passage into womanhood or where they met to prepare a girl before she was to be married.

I stood in the middle of the exposed patch of earth on top of the hill. It looked like a scar among the wild grasses and flowers. A community of birch trees stood watch over the old wound. It was the first time I walked the hill. Something had called me from the path around the pond, my usual walking trail. Barbed wire enclosed most of the hilltop, saying keep out. I had entered through a broken section in the fence. Snuck onto the land, a stealthy visitor.

The soles of my feet began to hum. I took a deep breath and held position. Vibration increased as if I stood on an electrical field. Harebells, what many would call bluebells, covered the hilltop, gently bending in the breeze. Taller flowers with big red centres like bulging buttons and yellow sunflower-like petals stood in the middle of the scar and dotted the hillside.

The hill told me a story and I saw it clearly: the teepees, the long dark hair of the women, and the deerskin dresses. I heard them laughing, a group of giggling girls, such love for one another as they caressed each other's hair with each stroke of the comb.

As I moved across the patch of earth — maybe four feet across and ten feet long, not clay or soil like the rest of the dirt, more like wet chalk — it felt as if someone was buried there. I stared at the earth. The tiniest ants moved in the longest line in perfect formation across the bald patch.

The scene returned. A deep knowing filled in the details. The First Nations community had come to the pond and the hillside in summer. They moved closer to the river in winter. I felt the energy through my soles, as if there was something there, just below the surface.

The railroad came and they moved, West perhaps. I stared at the train tracks below and the vast range of Rocky Mountains in the distance. I saw how the land looked before the trains. I stood in that time.

A great, great-grandmother, an elder-woman, was buried there in the patch where grasses didn't grow. The stand of red and yellow flowers marked her site. A visionary, a seer, she counselled the women and the community. She didn't know they'd left. She was suspended in a timeless place, waiting for their return in summer. She was still there: her spirit just beneath the soil.

Before I knew it, I had dropped to the earth and began to draw in the damp dirt: Sei He Ki, the Reiki symbol for emotional healing and to help those transition from one life to the next. I outlined the entire canvas of bare earth, using a small stick as my paintbrush. I leaned over to pick a single bell from a stand of harebell and place it on the patch to honour the elder but the whole stem came up: two full blossoms and one small and withered. The grave proved home to more than one soul.

I recited the Reiki symbol aloud — a puppet, the universe, my puppeteer — and lay the harebells on the ground as I stepped off the patch of exposed earth.

"They are not here anymore," I said. "They have gone. It is time for you to go too." The elder-woman with her long silver hair arose from below the surface with two younger women who joined her in the sky. Their shiny, long black hair merged with the silver of the great, great-grandmother as their spirits entwined into one.

Not one to ask for many things, particularly from the spirit of a First Nations elder, I suddenly requested her consideration of granting me a gift.

"Will you grace me with your gift of seeing," I blurted. "of vision?"

In the moments before she merged with the cosmos, I received no indication of her response.

My hands shook as the gravity of my request sank in. I had not meant to offend her or overstep. *Why did I ask that of her? I had no right to ask. But I need to know my purpose in life.*

ON MY KNEES *'fore you*
   Who AM I to set you free?
   Who AM I, not to?

2

NORMAL

Every night I walked. Between dinner and the kids' bedtime I walked around the pond. I entered the path on the northeast side of the water. That night a man walked his dog on the south side, heading in my direction. I recognized his energy. It was Leo. I met up with him and we walked together.

"Leo," I said, "have you ever had something happen and it makes no sense? Something that seemed so real to you when it was happening, but you knew it wasn't possible? Something *really* bizarre that had you saying *What the fuck*?"

"Yep," Leo replied. "Just tell yourself it's normal."

"What?" I stopped on the path and faced him.

"Just tell yourself it's normal. How do you know? Maybe it's normal. If you accept it as normal, there's no problem."

I was becoming familiar with Leo's approach to things: his stories with no endings, his simple solutions. They often frustrated the hell out of me, but I was becoming familiar with them all the same. Leo was a shaman. He was sixty-four years-old and his full head of fluffy grey and dark hair along with his weathered skin from time spent in the sun in the Southern States, made him appear Native American, though I believe his ancestry was Italian.

Leo had chosen a life of no fixed address, allowing Spirit to guide his way. He had a community of good friends both in Canada and the United States, and he spent months of the year in each. He had spent time with Native elders in both places but most of his stories were from time with his teacher in the South. He had been buried in the ground up to his neck, sealed in a cave, and walked the desert for days. Leo always gave me a different perspective, even if I had to fish the meaning from his stories.

I shared a few details of my experience on the hilltop, with the scarred earth and the elder woman. When I finished, Leo paused and said, "Hmmm, you are not done there. Go again."

We had circled the pond, crossed the road and climbed the hill back to our perspective homes. I gave Leo a hug and the dog a scratch on the head. I walked the remaining couple minutes to my backyard and stood, looking off to the mountains.

"Just tell yourself it's normal," I repeated Leo's words. What if it *is* normal?

WHOSE RULES HAVE I learned
  Nature holds her tongue no more
  I AM listening

3

TINY STORYTELLERS

Days before my vision on the hill, I had invited Leo over for tea and to give me a reading. He was house-sitting for my reiki friend, Sophie, who was on holiday with her family. Leo looked after her dog while she was away.

"What is my purpose?" I had asked him. "I mean, I know I'm to look after my family, write, and teach. I feel like there is something greater. Something I've not yet considered. Something I came here to do."

Leo shared yet another cryptic story with no ending. Probably something that went a lot like, "There is a duck. In a pond. There is a farmhouse across the field. You need to get to the farmhouse, but you can't fly. You're the duck. A man standing under a tree has a wheelbarrow. Inside is a teddy bear. The teddy bear is angry with you…" It was always for me to make sense of how the story applied to my situation and my question. Leo had little interest in explaining any of it. I liked that about his stories. His ego wasn't interested in deciphering his visions so that they made sense to me.

"Go outside every day and walk," he had ended our time together with this instruction.

I had sat in my yard that next day, ready for my walk. The new addition to my garden had caught my attention. I sat on the cool patio, eye level with the bright white wild anemones who had blown in one day and volunteered to cradle my stepping stones.

I suddenly remembered the exercise Leo had led our group through on the last day of my year in yoga, months earlier. He had taught us the practice of eye-gazing. It had had a profound effect on me that day and I decided to try it with one of the little white blossoms. I sat comfortably and engaged the bloom. Like star-gazing, I found myself deeply absorbed in plant-gazing.

I blinked when I needed to, and I held my gaze steady for what felt like ten or fifteen minutes. I was beginning to think about concluding the practice, no earth-shattering effects had emerged, when the petals began to glow. The entire blossom became luminous. The light extended past the petals like an herbal aura. I held my gaze fast to the light, so white it took on a bluish tinge, like the full moon on a clear night. I had no idea of the connection formed in that practice.

I had followed Leo's instructions and every day I walked, usually around the pond. Until that day, the day when I was pulled to walk up the hill. That day the flowers began to show me stories. Stories like that of the elder woman.

THE NEXT EVENING, after Leo had told me to return to the scarred earth, I walked along the path to the pond, intending to return to the hilltop. Instead I circled the pond and took up residence on an inlet in the middle. It's called Two-toed Pond because its shape resembles that of a deer's hoof print. I sat between the toes in meditation, watching the ripples of the wind on the water and the reflection of the homes on the ridge in the distance. I sat between the worlds of nature and man.

I stood to leave, not wanting to stay out too late, when I noticed feathers at my feet. I bent down to look at them. Normally I would take them home and plant them in my garden as prayer sticks, but they were small: the feathers of ducklings. I intended to leave them, when I felt compelled to place all four of them in my jacket pocket.

I headed across the road and started for the hill home. I was pulled in another direction. In fact, I stepped right off the path and began to find my own way through wild grasses across the lower ridge of the hillside. I dipped down into a small valley and stopped short, senses heightened, hairs on the back of my head prickled my scalp. I noticed a distinct change in not only vegetation but the feel of the land.

Several shrubs that I had never seen in the area squatted to one side. I saw a small pond or slough that did not exist. *This is normal*, I assured myself. I saw a farm or ranch just up from the slough. A house of settlers. Just then, a real red-winged blackbird flew to the top of one of the foreign bushes and screamed at me. I shivered. The area felt icky and dark, an energy I had yet to encounter, and if I lingered it would swallow me. I wanted to get out of there fast. I jumped over the lowest point in the valley, keeping my feet from making contact with this dark point in the earth, and quickly ascended the hill on the other side.

Harebells filled the hillside. There had been no flowers

in the tiny valley, but they flourished along the hill. The harebells became First Nations children, running, laughing, and playing in the grasses, heading for the water. A joyful summer day of play.

Out of nowhere, they were ambushed, the children cut down, along with the women who ran to their sides. No one saw it coming. The men were not there. I could not see who attacked. That information wasn't available to me. I sensed it was another band. Blood ran down the hillside as tears ran down my cheeks. I reached inside my pocket and felt something soft. I pulled out the four duckling feathers I had forgotten.

Re-enacting the ritual Leo had me perform when clearing the energy of my home weeks earlier, I addressed each of the four directions, offering a duckling feather to each in turn.

"There is no pain or sadness here," I said. "It is time to go home." The feathers drifted from my hand to the ground, along with my tears, and I continued to make my way up the hill. It seemed many more were trapped in time. Spirits solidified in the landscape.

The wind suddenly spoke, *Walk the coulee. All the way around.* I stopped to listen and tried to understand. How was I to walk the coulee? I'd visited stretches of the long stream in the narrow valley near my home. I wasn't even sure it could be done; if it was possible to travel the whole way around the community. Never mind the fact that it would take me the better part of a day, or more. The message was so firm I had to comply. I wasn't sure how or when, but I was sure I needed to follow the gale's instructions. I didn't want to stop whatever had started when I found the scarred hilltop and asked its elder-woman for her gift of vision.

· · ·

Walk, whispers the wind
　Move your feet across the earth
　Every cell complies

WE'RE NOT GOING AWAY

S teve and the kids came for a walk on a Saturday afternoon, an adventure through the coulee for my family. We took the path along the ridge with views of the mountains to the west and downtown Calgary to the east. We headed toward the city skyline. The sun stood high in the sky. At the end of the paved path we descended the steep hill into the coulee, away from neighbours and houses.

At the bottom, we found a small creek with great trees lining either side. A large, sturdy tree leaned over the water. Evidently popular with the locals, a thick, knotted rope hung from it: a playful way to cross to the other side.

Steve stretched his strong six-foot frame over the creek and pulled the rope to Michael. Eyes wide, the six-year-old grabbed onto the knotty handle and swung across the water, landing on the far bank. Steve helped Khali swing back and forth a few times before guiding her to the water's edge. He plucked the smiley near-three-year-old from the rope and set her down.

We decided to follow a small worn footpath along the

creek through the coulee. I had not taken that path before and marveled at the changes in scenery as we ventured forth. I felt as though I passed through many time periods and as many territories in one small coulee.

Birch trees dotted the hillsides and chickadees flew from branch to branch. We turned a corner and the temperature dropped as we slipped into the shade of tall evergreens that lined the creek and hill as if I'd stepped onto a mountain path. Further along and another corner gave way to rocky outcroppings and exposed geological layers topped with wild grasses, like slices of Earth's history on display. All the while the small creek babbled and chatted next to us.

Walking the path through the coulee, I began to plan the route for my homework assignment. I realized I could take my bike on the path and cover as much ground as possible in the three hour-window available with the kids in summer camp. I wouldn't be walking, as the wind requested, but it was the best I could do.

Michael and Khali came alive in the coulee. Walking the paved path on the ridge or to school produced endless complaining and dragging of feet, "I'm too tired to waaaaaaalk." Yet the earthy path winding through trees and alongside cool water energized the kids as they climbed rocks, jumped the stream, crossed back over on fallen trees and explored off-trail terrain. It was a grand adventure for them and for me. I soaked in the fresh air and the beauty of the landscape, feeling removed from the busy city streets.

Everywhere I saw flowers, I saw story. Three stunning red wood lilies, poised between two poplar trees on the opposite bank of the water, caught my attention. I paused while they morphed into First Nations women washing their hair in the stream. I gawked at the scene as Steve and the kids explored the trail ahead.

What surprised me in the coulee, more than the vast changing terrain and how we all came alive there, was that I could still see the stories with the kids and Steve present. I had assumed they were only available in silence and solitude. I felt as if I walked with one foot in one world and the other in a second, yet both seamlessly alive. I felt more and more at ease on the bridge between worlds. It was becoming normal.

WE SEE you see us
   Your eyes do not deceive you
   You asked for this world

FALLING FEAR

M ichael stretched his spine tall and pulled back his shoulders, inching the top of his head towards the *allowed to ride* line on the sign of the big roller coaster at the amusement park. Every year he tried for the elusive target and every year he fell short, to my relief. I despised roller coasters. They terrified me and always had.

"Maybe next year," I'd sing. Not this time. Michael stood just tall enough to gain entry to the coveted coaster. Of course, I sent Steve with him while Khali and I rode the safe, steady, scenic train on the outskirts of the park. As I cruised along with Khali, I contemplated the roller coaster and the possibility of conquering my fear. My mind filled with disappointment that I had sent Steve.

I wanted to try it. To see what would happen. Would I puke? Would I pass out? Would we have to leave the park because Mom got sick on the ride? I wanted to let go of my fear and at least try to conquer the feeling that I not-so-fondly remembered from childhood roller coaster rides at the fair: my stomach jumping into my lungs, no room for breath. I had held on to that memory of visceral fear since childhood and used it to keep me clear of repeating it.

Maybe it would be different. Maybe *I* was different. Maybe not. I wanted to find out. With all the self-inquiry, meditation, learning to breathe and let go, could I apply what I'd learned to one of my oldest fears?

Michael loved the roller coaster and wanted to go again. I decided to put pause to my panic and see if I could find joy buried beneath fear. I climbed into the roller coaster car and tugged on the seatbelts, ensuring we were both secure, twice. The car lurched forward and I made a conscious effort to loosen my death grip on the safety bar. I relaxed the tension in my belly and put all focus on my breath as we twisted and turned up and down hills. *Breathe, just breathe.*

We slowly crested the big hill, one rung at a time, *clack, clack, clack*. I drew a deep, deliberate breath as we neared the top. Suspended at the peak, both car and breath: the calm before the storm. We plunged along the rails toward the bottom. My stomach found my lungs, but it was met with breath and I felt energized, not faint, as I purposefully exhaled. We approached the signature inverted loop. Again, an enlivening inhale. I let go of the bar and threw my hands overhead in surrender as I felt gravity take a new position. My scream turned to laughter as I found not only joy buried beneath the long-time fear, but also freedom.

"Again! Again!" I heard as the car pulled into the off-loading area. It wasn't Michael's voice that shouted, it was mine. I helped him off the ride, beaming from ear to ear.

I was primed for more and we headed to *The Drop*, the ride that lifts rows of people to the top of a tower, over-looking the amusement park and the fields, and then drops them, stopping inches before the ground only to pull them all back up for another drop. My stomach churned at the thought but the high from the roller coaster egged me on. Michael and I strapped in and the operator raised the seated platform to the top of the frame. Hawks flew near. I realized the enormity of the tree across the pond as I now looked upon its top branches.

W*hoomp,* I clutched the bar. My stomach leapt into my chest, no time to breathe. Do-over. We slowly repeated the climb. This time I took a deep breath, lifting my hands from the bar and my feet in the air, releasing my tightly-held belly and shoulders with the exhale. *Whoomp,* we dropped again. This time *I* directed the breath.

With each drop I relaxed more, accepting the free-fall and letting go of my control of anything. I was in control of nothing, other than this breath, and the next, and the next. I watched the hawks on the breeze and the top of the great tree reaching for the sun, giving shade to park patrons below. I took another breath and another. Freedom and joy applauded.

I soared with the hawks. I rose above the tallest of trees. I took a leap and the only thing that fell that day was fear.

You show me struggle
  lead me to dark, closed spaces
  that I may open

THE WOMAN IN DEERSKIN

"There is a Native woman at your sacred place," said Leo. I met with him again before he finished his house-sit for Sophie.

"My sacred place?" I asked.

"Your hill," he replied.

I had never thought of it as my sacred place but as he said it, I felt privileged to have such a place, where few others visited and where the land first shared its stories with me.

"She is wearing red and deerskin and wants to meet with you. She has information for you if you ask the right question. If not, she will leave and never come back. She will wait a while for you to come. Don't wait too long," he said.

"If I ask the right question? What kind of mind-fuck is that?" I exploded at him. "That's going to send my head into outer space, trying to figure out the *right* question. Thanks a lot." Leo and I had gotten to know each other since my year in yoga and I cherished our friendship. I could talk to Leo about anything supernatural and he never flinched, judged, or blew smoke up my ass. I kidded him about his stories with no endings and the cryptic Native-style wisdom that reminded me of Zen proverbs: the inquiry happens during the mind's struggle with the proverb, not the actual understanding of the meaning.

That's what appealed to me most about working with Leo: he may lead me to water, but it was up to me to drink. I thought I wanted someone to tell me what I needed to do, what my purpose was, what I needed to heal, or how to find happiness. Whenever someone did, however, it didn't ring true. It felt like *their* information, their truth, their perspective, their wisdom. I wanted my own.

"Why First Nations?" I asked.

"What do you mean?"

"I'm white. Who am *I* to connect with this energy? I never asked for it."

"The land has stories. These stories belong to all of us. You don't get to choose."

Working with Leo helped me get my feet on the path and then left me to the work of walking the path, arriving at my destination in my own time. Whenever that happened for me, when I received insights, wisdom and ah-ha moments, they felt true. As much as his deerskin woman in red frustrated me, I knew I was on the verge of a discovery and the only struggle was mine if I chose it. And boy did I choose it.

I wrestled with what question to ask. I went back and forth between letting go of my need to find the perfect question (allowing it to surface) and making a concerted effort to think of what needed to be asked. *What if the whole point of the exercise is to let go of the need to ask the right question? That would be a Leo-thing. But what if it isn't and I waste the opportunity to receive valuable personal guidance?*

Days passed. Contrary to my usual reaction, I didn't run

right out and jump on the new opportunity. I waited, hoping clarity would come and a question would form.

With both kids in camp I finally made the walk to the hilltop. I asked permission to enter, laid my jacket down on the scar on the earth and sat on it. I could still make out the lines I had drawn of the reiki symbol. I sat inside it and waited quietly, feeling in the silence for the woman in deerskin and red.

I thanked her for coming and then something happened I didn't expect. All my composure — my feelings of privilege to receive the honour of this question, this meeting, this wisdom — it all left me. I started to cry.

"I don't know what to ask. I don't know what's happening or how to respond or live in this way. I feel alone in this and don't know how to make my way in it. I just want to be happy and my family to be healthy. I want to understand what else exists and I can't make any sense of it. I don't know who I am or what I am supposed to do here. I feel sad by the state of the world and want desperately to help but I feel so small. I am sorry." I dropped my head. "I do not know the right question."

I was shaking and blubbering by the end. Tears streamed down my face and I watched them drop onto the clay, mixing with the dust and earth as I waited for her to fade away. I felt a great softening and then the opening of a door. I felt her presence draw closer to comfort me. Information streamed toward me as fast and plentiful as my tears streamed away. Messages and answers, insights and direction. None of it coherent, yet all of it understood.

After what felt like hours of purging and downloading simultaneously, I felt empty of grief and sadness, and content with comfort. I was not handed some grand purpose nor was I given a title or job description or the key to the end of suffering and struggle. I was given simple, gentle understanding of where I was at that moment and that period of my life. Of the steps I could choose to take, the stepping stones that allowed me to move patiently and slowly through that time.

I was in school and the land was my teacher. My assignment was to master my visions, hear the stories being told, and then share their wisdom with others. Re-membering. I understood that different dimensions existed at once and it was in the ability to move within these different dimensions that great healing could occur, karmic healing. What I didn't know was if these dimensions existed externally, internally, or both.

I saw how I walked around my neighbourhood, lived in my home with my family, unaware of what the land around me had seen, what the people who walked and lived on it before me had endured. Sacrifice and suffering had occurred, and the land retained the memory, imprinted in the soil and inherited by the flowers. The plants kept the story and held the medicine to ease past pain and heal future struggle. I assumed the timeline at the time. What I didn't understand was that dreamtime, the realm of visions, had its own time: no time.

I was an eager student, willing to learn, and the visions held powerful, emotional and connective energy for me. I felt more at home in the visions, and the stories helped me feel more at home in the world around me. I felt connected to the most kind, loving and immense force and although I could not describe it, identify or name it, I knew wholeheartedly, with all that I was, that I wanted dearly to remain connected to it. It seemed to know me, and I wanted to know it.

The journey to my sacred place was never about what

the woman in deerskin and red had to tell me. I thought if I was intuitive enough, if I was psychic enough, she would give me the answer, the one thing that revealed my purpose, the secret to my life. It wasn't about her answer. It was about what unfolded in my mind as I struggled to find the perfect question. It was about knowing my mind and watching it grasp for answers. It was about gathering the courage to meet her, and trust that the question would arise. And it was about allowing myself the vulnerability to break down in humility, in my own nakedness and rawness, cracked open and pouring my confusion and suffering onto the soil. It was about baring my broken soul to the earth, witnessing and feeling my pain. It was about healing myself along the way.

*H*UMBLE *WARRIOR*

Stained glass armour forged in fire
Shattered on the earth

7

AN HISTORICAL RACE

E very night I slept near a two-thousand-year-old teepee ring. The foundation stones were discovered in my community during development, along with another archaeological site, home to arrows, bowls and animal remains dating back ten-thousand years. The teepee ring location was supposedly marked. I desperately wanted to find it, as if sitting within it might provide answers to the visions, the stories of the land and my purpose. I was sure I would come across it on my bike ride around the community.

Walk the coulee. All the way around. Summer camp only afforded me a few hours without kids. I knew I couldn't cover that much ground walking and opted to take my bike. *It'll have to do.* I grabbed a grocery bag from my pantry and tossed in my water bottle, journal, pen, and two granola bars. I hung the bag from my handlebar.

Immediately upon hitting the trail the story began to unfold. The flowers became people. Different species for different people. The red wood lilies were the women, the harebells, children. I saw the elders and the hunting parties.

It was as if I biked through a small English town during a theatre festival. I pedaled along from stage to stage, each play rich with characters, costumes and story. I stopped to watch the performance, jotted down the details, and then biked on to view the next play, and the next.

I saw children running and playing in the wild grasses. I saw horses drinking from a meadow pond. I saw the hunting party and their gathering site. I saw a deer that wasn't there and warned it of the hunting party. I saw where the marriages took place and where the new couple made their bed. I saw where everyone gathered to share a meal. And I mapped it all: a cartographer of story.

Like a Disney tale: the dragonflies became horses, the fireweed and wood sage became men, the wolf-willow became the scenery that set the story. I became the witness, the scribe, and perhaps, one day, the storyteller.

Wolf-willow, silverberry bush, something happens to me every time I catch the scent on the breeze: a memory etched in my DNA. You might smell cinnamon and it reminds you of your Grandma's apple pie and in that moment you are transported to her kitchen. That is me and wolf-willow. Only, the memory doesn't exist in this life. The fragrance is a thread that tethers me to Spirit. It reminds me how many lifetimes I have walked the earth. It's a friend who accompanies me on this walk.

The sweet scent sustains me. It soothes my soul and I know its origin to be powerful even if I can't recall the memory. My soul knows it. And I wait every spring for it. And I stand at my open window when the breeze comes from the west and I smell deeply, inhaling over and over again, as if unable to sufficiently saturate my cells with the aromatherapy. This is my fuel, the replenishing of my energy. I offer every available breath as I drink deeply from this aromatic well, knowing it will leave as summer approaches and I will wait another year for its perfume. When I die, it is the scent of the wolf-willow I will follow home.

In the far northwest corner of the community, where a large undeveloped space remained, covered in wild grasses with few flowers, I stopped. Busy roads intersected this corner. A small tree nursery called it home. A series of towering electrical poles ran the length of one side. There was no stage here, no vibrant display. There was disruption. I felt agitated. The sound was deafening.

What is that? A steady hum. Not pleasing. A chaotic chorus of crickets. The land felt unsettled. I paused to go within and find what was needed of me to help this place. *What happened here?* I waited for an answer, a sense or a scene. Nothing came. *It's beyond me.* Despite my desire to heal the agitation in the land, there was nothing for me to do in this place. Saddened, I took a deep breath and surrendered to the power that compelled me. And I left.

As I biked along a roughly worn trail on the outskirts of the community, feeling pressed for time, I thought about squeezing in my sacred place. That would connect the energy full circle around the community. I really didn't have enough time to add the extra distance and get back to pick up the kids on time. I deemed the sacred work more important, however, and pressed on. I blazed my own trail down a large grassy hill, heading for the paved path below.

It looked as if I could make the final drop from the hillside to the path. At the last second, I realized it was steeper than I thought, and I tried to turn parallel to the hillside for a more gradual approach to the pavement. Too late. My bike flipped sideways, and I headed for the asphalt and a hard fall.

Thoughts flew through my head as I flew through the air: *I need to pick the kids up from camp... I am at the end of the path... no one will hear me or help me... this is going to be bad ...I don't have time to walk the bike home if it is damaged.*

I lay beneath the bike frame on the pavement and nervously scanned my body. I felt only minor pain and a bit shook up. I pushed the bike off me and stood to see how I could have possibly survived the fall without major injury. A perfect thick layer of tall grasses leaned over the path directly beneath me. They had folded over from the hillside, providing a grassy bed on which to land. I sustained a couple bruises from the bike frame, none from the pavement as the grass had caught my fall. It was a miracle I hadn't broken bones.

You can't force this, Steph. Nature may be your teacher, but clearly, she won't let you abandon your life's duties. In fact, it was as if Nature knew my agenda, and worked to help me. I picked up my bike, made it home to grab the car and precisely on time to meet the kids. If I'd continued, I'd have been exceedingly late, stranding my kids at camp. I never found the teepee ring.

A RACE between worlds
Pulled in two in search of one
Nature holds my hand

8

A NEAR MISS WITH MURDER

Determined to pick up the trail, I veered off course. I opted to walk through my neighbourhood instead of past the pond. I chose the most direct route to the dead-end paved path where I had crashed my bike the previous day. I intended to complete the loop around the community and end at my sacred place. I passed through rows of houses and walked along the path, winding down into the trees and valley.

My community perched on the edge of the city. Parts felt distinctly urban then led to rural, wild areas with tall grasses, treed coulee and majestic distant mountains. I passed between a grassy hill and a long, orderly grove of birch trees. A tremendous ruckus rocked the distance: crows, not a few but what sounded like a mob.

I could see one of the nearby golf course fairways. Stepping off the path and continuing on the grass up the hill between the golf course and the community would eventually take me to my sacred place, my intended destination. I wanted to sit there and meditate after my long walk. The grassy hillside dropped down into a deeper valley between me and the golf course. I couldn't see over the hill and into the steep valley. Trees camouflaged the lower hillside.

I rounded the corner of the paved path, reaching the end, the place where I had crashed my bike. I could see the crows, gathered on the arms of a giant power pole: an ineffective metal scarecrow on the top of the hill toward my sacred place. As I stepped off the pavement heading up the hill, the crows went crazy, all of them cawing at once. They took off and headed over my head in the opposite direction to where I was going.

I stopped dead in my tracks, stunned by the flapping scrum. They collectively perched on the roof of a house up the path behind me. The size of the group alone commanded attention. I'd never seen such a large murder of crows. I counted them, as they sat still on the roof, thirty-two. They seemed to be trying to get my attention. I stood between the crows on the rooftop and the hill to my sacred place. I turned toward the hill and the crows went crazy again, shrieking and yelling. I turned back toward them and stepped onto the path, heading in their direction. They went silent.

They all took flight, moving several houses back up the path and perching again on a rooftop, not too far as to lose my attention but far enough to lure me back up the path. I walked toward them. A grassy hill stood between the crows and me. I couldn't have been closer than fifty feet at any given time. I posed no threat to them. They didn't seem to be running away from me as much as they appeared to be leading me away from the hill and my sacred place.

I neared the house and they once again flew to the roof of another, this time taking me off the walking path and back into the neighbourhood. I paused a moment, thinking about my plan to complete the loop and reach my sacred place. I had brought my journal and pen, hoping to receive another vision or inspiration or be audience to another great story. *Perhaps I'm not welcome today.* I continued to follow the captivating crows.

A comical site, I'm sure: the crows leading their human pet along the path on a morning walk. Their behaviour fascinated me. How could I not oblige? They led me up the sidewalk to the main street near Michael's school and a shortcut home. Then they all flew at once, heading north and out of sight, leaving me at the school. I decided to head home and jot down the odd event, no sacred place for me this day.

I loved the coulee and living on the edge of the city. Large families of deer moved across the hillsides and along the pond. Coyotes came up from the river valley and made dens in the grassy hills. A giant peaceful porcupine ambled through the ravine in search of good eats, emerging in the fall for the neighbour's apple tree. Even a pair of beavers had found their way in and went to work damming the creek. I felt as if I lived surrounded by nature within an urban community and I loved that.

Like most communities, interesting news travelled fast, and I received an email the following day: a police warning. It appeared a young black bear was seen the day before, heading to the golf course. Its path would have precisely intersected mine.

I burst into laughter. I couldn't help myself and I couldn't help but think possibly thirty-two of nature's black-feathered boy scouts had led me from inadvertently star-tling our furry visitor. I would have crested the hill on my silent walk, putting both me and the bear in a precarious position. I thanked my noisy scouts and decided to pay closer attention to nature's behaviour. Even if her messages conflicted with my plans.

I headed over to Sophie's to say goodbye to Leo. It was time for him to move on to his next house-sit. Sophie returned home later in the day, and as happy as I was to see her, I was sad for Leo to go. My meetings with him and our walks, his stories and guidance, helped me feel connected to something greater. He had helped me re-connect to nature and open to story, creativity, vision, possibility, imagination, and healing.

But after that day, life got busy and I felt tired from all the stories I'd been told. I didn't know what to do with the information, the map I drew the day I biked the coulee, or the experience. I stopped walking. I took a rest.

NATURE IS alive
   Always in conversation
   Listen up!

9

NATURE'S APPRENTICE

The initiation from my plant-gazing with the white blossom combined with my time with Leo opened up the doors of Nature's school. I didn't realize I was changing classes as one of my teachers left and another was about to appear. Tired, I spent more time indoors, listening to the birds and sounds outside. The birds became impatient with me and began to call me out.

The magpies squawked loudly. I sat at the kitchen table, writing. They kept calling. I tried to focus on the page in front of me. Raaaawh. Raaaaawh. Rawh rawh. I finally complied, left my writing and headed out the back door, following them a short distance up the path.

"If there is nothing by the time I get to the top of this hill," I scolded them, "I'm going back inside." They all took off once I reached the top. Two majestic bald eagles glided effortlessly on the thermals in an ancient spiral. I had never seen bald eagles that close. The two of them, in a choreographed dance on the wind, lifted my heart with them. I was so excited by the sight, I ran barefoot down the path to Sophie's, and knocked on her door. She popped out of a reiki session to answer and was equally delighted by the eagle sighting. We watched them soar off east from her front step. I returned indoors, to my tea and my computer.

THE NEXT DAY, with Michael at summer camp, Khali jumped in the little red wagon and I pulled her on a walk to my sacred place. I would have normally gone alone but I had little available time before we headed on our annual family holiday to the mountains. I wanted to visit my sacred place before we left. I hadn't been since the encounter with the woman in red.

A large orange butterfly met us on the path near the site and escorted us in. I left the wagon near the opening in the old barbed wire fence that once marked the land as someone's. I assumed it was part of the community's holdings, but it still could have belonged to one of the few remaining farms down the hill.

An even larger brown and orange butterfly welcomed us at the fence and led us to the scar in the earth. Khali loved the butterflies and wildflowers. She explored the local creepy-crawlies among the wild grasses.

"Do you have a question?" came the soft voice of the woman in deerskin and red, who apparently remained available to me.

"I feel as if I am stuck and should be doing something. What should I be doing?" I asked.

"Come back outside," she replied.

Day after day, I'd been sitting in my house at my laptop, hoping to find direction. Sitting inside my four walls had kept me tuned into my computer. My direction didn't appear to be found there. Standing at my sacred place with

Khali, the woman in deerskin and red let me know that it was time to return to daily walking and tune back into nature.

∾

THE FOLLOWING day we made the picturesque drive to our favourite mountain getaway. I noticed yoga on the resort itinerary, offered both alongside the main river in the heart of the property and up the chairlift on the mountainside. I opted for mountainside yoga and took the chairlift early the next morning while Steve slept in with the kids.

I headed for the wooden observation deck at the top of the lift: the meeting space for morning yoga. The first to arrive, I watched the lift and observed the others en route to class with the teacher. Save the instructor, everyone had a good twenty-years on me. I decided to make a quick getaway and leave the group to enjoy their own class.

It's not that I wouldn't have enjoyed yoga with the group. Okay, maybe it was that I wouldn't have enjoyed yoga with the group. I wanted to move energy in a big way and my spidey-senses told me that class was going to move at a tourist pace.

I grabbed my water bottle and snuck off along the trail behind the platform before anyone noticed me, cutting through the grass-carpeted ski hills. I intended to continue to the clearing on the far side of the trail, but an orange butterfly caught my eye. She flew along beside me. She passed me and stopped in the middle of the trail, settling herself on the ground.

I decided to follow her lead and placed my water bottle on the earth near her, removing my sandals. It seemed a strange place to do morning yoga, on the path in the trees between two large openings, but a small creek trickled along next to me and the sun's rays angled directly toward me. I began to flow in sun salutations, growing warmer with each one and the rising sun. I removed my sweater, placing it on the ground as a makeshift mat for earth postures.

I was alone on the mountainside, removed from the observation deck class. I felt a presence there, not that of the wind or birds: I kept feeling bear. It occurred to me my decision to do yoga alone on a Rocky Mountain hillside may have not been the wisest. I settled with the lingering bear presence and subsequent fear, and remained alert during my practice.

My senses heightened on the mountain. I stood in tree pose, face-to-bark with a tall, twisty friend. I extended my own branches skyward as I sank my roots deep into the mountain soil. I welcomed the sun on my face and the birds as my neighbours.

I completed my practice in seated meditation, a part of nature, melded into the mountainside. The heat on my face brought me out of bliss as the summer sun strengthened. I pulled a cloth from my bag. I had placed a few drops of essential oil onto it before leaving the hotel room that morning. I brought it to my face for a deep draw of the invigorating blend: rose and pine, warm and alive.

I took my cloth to the creek and soaked up the icy mountain water, placing the cloth over my face. The cold stung my skin. The scent stirred my spirit. I could not recall a more rejuvenating spa treatment. I felt perfect and complete and alive. I wanted to drink from the stream. *That can't be safe, you could get sick drinking from a stream.*

The pull to drink outweighed the conditioning to not drink from the wild water source and I cupped my hands together, scooping water up to my mouth. I ingested the pure, cold, mountain life force. I tingled from head to toe, every cell alive and awake.

I reluctantly gathered my things, slowly tying my sweater around my waist, and dawdled back along the trail. I crossed the ski hill to the chair lift, pausing behind a grove of trees to ensure the class had completed before I emerged from behind them. The resort had woken since my practice and people began to gather at the lift, making their hiking and biking plans for the day.

A small crowd huddled near a wooden billboard. I hadn't noticed the signage on my way up. I walked over to see what it said. It was the day's bear sightings, warning hikers to plan their routes accordingly. The first sighting of the day was recorded at about the same time I arrived at my yoga location on the trail. The map showed the bear had enjoyed her berries in the meadow just uphill from the end of the trail where I practiced. Had I not stopped with the butterfly, continuing instead to the opening, I'd have been the bear's guest for breakfast.

There are several wild animals one would not like to encounter in the woods of the Rockies, however, most pose no real threat, at least not that I have ever felt. Except bear. I like to say I have a healthy respect for bears. I love them. They are beautiful, strong and gentle creatures. It is, perhaps, the one animal I truly fear coming face to face with in the wild. Although I love spotting them, I am not certain an encounter would leave me intact.

There are many books written on animal totems. A shaman teacher of mine, in later years, said the best way to understand the energy of an animal that has entered your life, is to study its behaviour. What does the animal eat? What are its sleeping, waking and socialization patterns? What was it doing at the time you encountered the animal?

What does it mean to you? This is where you will find the truth of an animal's message.

Bear is often misunderstood, even by me. Bear is strong and quick, but also playful and gentle. Bear hibernates in the winter, a time for deep rest and reduced activity. Bear is challenged by few other animals. She is protective. She is content alone on a mountain hillside in the warm rays of the sun. She simply wants to be left in peace.

Twice in one month my path came near bear, and both times nature safely guided me. The first required an entire murder of crows to convince me to alter my route. The second required only the gentle encouragement of a butterfly. Summer school began to show its lessons. I was becoming an adept student.

To KNOW your meaning
  your purpose on this planet
  come to your senses

10

FALL REGISTRATION IS NOW OPEN

I hadn't shared my nature school experiences with anyone other than Leo. I couldn't imagine who would be open to *that* conversation. I appeared to be the sole student in the system, at least in my neck of the woods.

With September well underway, I finally had a chance to catch up with my dear friend Anna via phone. We had much to say and an upcoming trip to Sedona to plan. It was meant to cap off our year in yoga: the journey of that year with Anna and Alora fills *An Accidental Awakening*. Our whole community was supposed to experience the red rocks with Alora as our guide since she'd led our year-long yoga inquiries. When our year had come to completion, however, travelers dropped like flies, including Alora. Anna and I had decided to keep our commitment and make the journey together at the time of our birthdays in fall. Scorpio sisters, Anna's birthday landed on October 30th, while mine was November 3rd. She would turn forty-seven, and me, thirty-nine.

It seemed late to be seeking my life's purpose. Then again, prior to my spiritual awakening, I had no desire to find it. There was an urgency now: a compulsion to be of benefit to the world: to know my place on the planet.

I paced back and forth across the living room carpet, gazing out the window at the mountains in the distance. I paced when I was excited and when there was a lot to say. And Anna and I had a lot to say.

"Spiritual discovery has a lightning pace," she commented, and I nodded.

I made up my mind not to disclose my nature studies with her just yet. I needed to get clearer on the purpose of my nature walks first.

"Stephy, every experience I had this summer led to another even more fascinating than the last. It's like a trail of cosmic breadcrumbs."

I continued to pace, listening to her words and the hushed excitement in her voice, as if speaking the experiences aloud diminished their power.

"I just finished an incredible book," she continued. "The author shares his experiences with clearing the energy of land through ritual walks."

I stopped pacing, my feet anchored to the carpet.

"Anna," I gasped. "You need to hear what I've been doing."

And then it all poured out: the strange events and stories that had unfolded on the land around my community. I spoke so fast I don't think I took a breath.

"Forward me the name of the author," I said. "And the title of his book."

She sent it as soon as we ended our call. I searched online immediately upon receipt of Anna's email. The author, originally from Mexico, just happened to live in Calgary. *What?* He taught at our main college and offered his own services as well. *What are the odds of that? He lives in my city.*

I surfed between the pages of the college and his private work. He offered a course for the fall. I emailed him, revealing briefly the guided walks around my community. I asked if I should take his course or book a private session with him. I had no idea what I would say, only that I knew he could shed light on the events of my summer. He replied with an offer of a silent walk together.

Hello Stephanie:

It is nice to hear from you.
I have availability to see you next Friday at 10 am. Please set a meeting place and confirm.

Warm regards,
Fernando Davalos

"The West admires those that push their way to the top and the Indigenous Traditions of the world admire those who leave their egos behind."

So GOES the saying
    When the student is ready
    the teacher appears

11

THE CALL

I had many questions for Fernando and although grateful for his offer to walk with me, I wondered how he would answer my questions during our silent walk. We parked in a lot near Calgary's reservoir, host to a variety of walking and cycling paths. We introduced ourselves. I trembled slightly, nervous to convey my gratitude for his generous offer. I always seemed to lose a little of my own power when I stood in the presence of powerful teachers, no matter how humble they were.

We moved to a small circle of trees where Fernando said a blessing. I tried to suppress my discomfort. It wasn't the blessing that made me feel itchy. It was the stream of cyclists, dog-walkers, and joggers passing by our spruce sanctuary. I tried to focus on Fernando's words, but my discomfort amplified the sounds of bike bells and barking dogs.

We made off down the path in complete silence. I struggled to walk with him that way. I reminded myself of unimposed silence, something I'd learned during my recent year in yoga. The simple suggestion of *unimposed* helped me relax rather than working to force silence. Fernando appeared comfortable with the quiet and I worried my busy mind might be obvious and distracting to him. I had questions. I hoped for answers.

We passed others on the busy paths. I noticed how strongly I felt the compulsion to greet them. I resisted my usual sing-songy *good morning* or *hello*. I tried not to make eye contact but felt like I was being rude. *Should I nod?* I settled on a genuine smile. We left the paved path and began along a graveled foot-path through the trees.

Fernando ahead of me, my rhythmic step on the earth, the bird songs and the leaves gently chatting in the breeze: all brought me in tune with the hours I had spent silent walking around my neighbourhood. I noticed a squirrel dart from tree branch to tree branch like my mind darted from thought to thought and then I fell in step with Fernando. For a few moments it was as if we walked as one.

We neared a clearing, a large meadow, and my palms began to tingle. Heat moved through them as it did in a reiki session with the kids or a client. I wanted to stop moving and allow the energy session with the meadow to continue. A gap in the trees let me see the clearing. I stared at the open space with tall grasses, opening my mind and senses to what was there. Heat flowed freely from my hands.

A squirrel chatted loudly behind me. The distance had grown between Fernando and me. I hastened my step to lessen the gap.

We continued on and I began to notice the trees, not the landscape in general but a few specific trees that stood out like elder trees: tall, evergreens with heavy, reaching branches: sturdy trees that obviously had weathered many storms and stood up to the strong chinook winds. I felt their watchful gaze as we moved through their land.

We arrived at a giant of a tree with a thick trunk. Fernando approached, placing both hands on the strong trunk. He stood for a long time communing with what seemed like an old friend. He moved away and I stepped up to the tree offering my hands to its trunk, uncertain of what I was to feel or think or intend.

"Would you like to take a small meditation here?" asked Fernando, breaking the silence.

"Yes," I replied, unsure what my other options were and not ready to make the return silent trip. We took up positions on logs and rocks near the river and closed our eyes. I didn't expect much since I felt awkward meditating with Fernando, clearly an adept teacher and meditator. I felt keenly aware that his clear mind could see my busy mind. *Paranoia*, I reassured myself.

Not new to meditation, I knew I was a rookie compared to the reverent man seated across from me. *Does he see strange visions? Does he talk to unseen worlds? Does the land also tell him stories?* I decided my questions may not be answered that day and settled into my earthy seat to enjoy the sounds and smells of Glenmore Reservoir. The river swirled and curled at the bank's edge behind me. A shaded earthy enclave sheltered a thin layer of ice, formed from a cold fall night. The whirling waters played the ice like a xylophone, lulling me into daytime dreamtime.

A massive tree appeared before me: the Bodhi tree, Buddha's tree. Many paths led to it. Then no paths. Just me and the tree. Then I became the tree, and I understood the seasons of life.

Rooted in the earth, the soil fed me. The rain and rivers nourished and cleansed me. The sun helped me grow, burning away old growth to make way for new. The air sustained me and the wind restored me.

I grew uncomfortable on my log and shifted. Taking a deep breath, I opened my eyes.

"We are very small, you and I," Fernando said. "If someone like the Dalai Lama walked through these paths, everyone would come. They would be drawn to this place. We hear *the call*. The earth needs healing and you and I hear the call. We offer our help. We offer what we can and in that offering others more powerful than us come to help. Some powerful people can change the weather; can bring rain, can evoke great change, but there must first be a call."

I listened to his words with my whole body, absorbing them into my cells. When the birds called me outside, I often witnessed a magnificent event, like eagles soaring. When I walked quietly, I heard the call of the earth, the pull of nature school, and magical stories spread out on the land before me.

When I listened for the call, I received instructions on what to do and how to help. My lessons were easy. When I strained to be clever, to work without the call, lessons were often difficult, if available at all.

When I applied the law of the call and listened for it from those around me, nature, and from deep within — in dreamtime, meditation or revealed through my sadness and joys — life flowed easier. When I applied the law of the call I felt most in service to the earth and to others. When I heard the call, walking the land or in ceremony, insight arrived, and my senses expanded exponentially. All that was needed for the call, was to listen; be quiet and listen with my whole body.

When I waited for the call everything I needed to proceed fell into place. Sometimes I made the call, asking the universe for help. Thankfully others listened and responded to support me. I would eventually come to appreciate the patience and vigilance required to not act until first there was a call. And to let go of the demand for a call at all.

"This area was once a training ground for the military," Fernando continued, and I thought back to the heat in my hands as I passed the meadow. I could only imagine the energy that military training exercises brought to a land. Fernando had answered my question about what had happened there without me asking. It seemed the area needed TLC. Perhaps sometimes you don't hear the call; you feel it.

UNIMPOSED SILENCE
Presence the seasons of life
The call will find you

12

REAL LIFE OR FANTASY

Failing to find the elusive teepee ring gnawed at me. I mentioned it casually to a friend in the community one day. She said she knew where it was. Her daughter's class had visited it. Of *course* she had, because that's how life works. Apparently, I had needed to meet with Fernando before I could meet with the teepee ring. She described the location and I noted it in my mind.

In the coming days, I took up Fernando's work. Merging his practice with my walks, I cleared my head while I cleared the land around my community. Most days, I walked the hillsides nearest me. They felt comfortable and welcoming. When I ventured out into territory unknown, I would encounter areas that felt constricted and heavy. As I returned again and again to walk them, they began to lighten.

I dropped the kids at school one day and headed to my sacred place to meditate. I missed sitting with the land on my hilltop and my pace quickened with excitement as I approached the barbed wire fence. I greeted my sacred place like an old friend, two giddy girls excited to catch up. I sat in the centre of the scar and closed my eyes.

Immediately they surrounded me. I sat in a circle of ancestors. A large tribe sat to my left. An elder took up position behind me and tingling ran up and down my spine like I was being attuned to the land. I sat in the circle and received nature's healing session, oblivious to time and space. Neither existed. I was suspended in a formless field of sensory excitement, every cell dancing. No thoughts existed. I experienced my environment, internal and external, on a heightened plane with ecstatic joy while electrical shocks coursed through my veins and skin.

A swelling emerged from deep within as gratitude welled inside me and burst open the gates of my heart. Tears filled my eyes as I was both humbled and exalted at once. I thanked my tribe who I wanted to know more of, to understand as real. I wanted to Google the history of my community and find the same faces I saw on the hill captured in print in the history books. Somehow that would make it real for my mind. I could then justify my experiences, call them psychic visions or identify them as channeling spirits.

I knew that would not happen. The visions were gifted on trust, as lessons to open me to great story, possibility, healing, and redefining *normal*. It was all part of a greater creative process and a deeper guiding force.

Maybe the elder woman didn't exist, but the vision caused me to draw an enormous ancient healing symbol on the scarred land. Maybe the woman in deerskin and red didn't exist. But the encounter forced me to face my fears and pain and expose myself to healing while tears blessed the earth.

Maybe the children were never slaughtered on the hillside. But the painful sight compelled compassion and understanding from me, along with the sacred ceremony of the four directions. Maybe it was all fantasy. But the fantasy enticed me to engage in sacred traditions. Traditions of healing and caretaking that have been forgotten, neglected or never known to many: held by wisdom keepers, modern society remiss to include or even consider the extent of their reach. Maybe my experience was normal. Maybe it was real.

Whatever the truth, I felt the magnitude and deep healing of the experiences. I gave up searching to prove that what I saw existed. I accepted it as my unique passage and allowed it to draw me into deeper communion with myself, the land, and Spirit.

PAST, present, future
    Simultaneous healing
    Timeless illusion

13

A MAGICAL RING

While most mothers dropped their kids at school and headed to work or the gym, got their hair done, loaded the laundry or shopped for groceries, I sought out sacred places with great anticipation of communing with nature, speaking with elder ancestors and experiencing states of bliss. It was, indeed, *my normal*.

I walked to the teepee ring to conduct an awakening ritual of the energy of my community as a sacred site. I'm not entirely sure where I got the idea to do it but most certainly the seed was planted on one of my walks. I tried not to think about it because if I did the thoughts went something like: *What the hell is going on? Go home and do laundry and yoga. Who am I to conduct sacred ceremonies – skinny, white chick.*

If Fernando hadn't dared to follow *his* call and share his wisdom and insights with others, I would have ceased to continue my pursuits. For someone, a teacher, to come along and say, *what you're doing is something we've been doing for centuries, longer than centuries*, it provided the permission

I needed to continue. I craved every moment of it: more visions, more insights, more ecstasy, more tearful gratitude and unseen councils. I felt at home.

Like a proud student completing my practicum, I approached the teepee ring with all my tools. I asked permission to enter and drew upon the practices Leo had shared with me. Fernando had said that a great healing formula for the land was to take someone of the lineage of those who did harm and, with great respect, perform the traditions of those who had been harmed. It was equally clarifying and gratifying to receive affirmation of the practices I had carried out over the summer. I continued to merge Leo's traditional practices with my *colonial* energy, to provide the alchemy for honouring the land and clearing past karma.

It was not in disrespect of my own ancestors. It was in reverent acknowledgment of healing and the oneness of all life. That healing is more important than blame. Most importantly, I followed the guidance that arose from my deep, loving union with the land.

Most lands witnessed a range of human emotions and actions. In my community people went about their day, driving and stepping where ancient civilization once hunted and celebrated. Where agreements were made, where land changed hands, where tribes were pushed aside and where lines were drawn and crossed, reinforced and fenced off.

I am not an expert on First Nations culture, on the history of my province, or the events of the early settlers. I do know, growing up in my community, the division between cultures, particularly the First Nations and white cultures. I grew up in rural Alberta. I attended a school of two hundred kids from kindergarten to grade twelve. I knew of no racial issues because I grew up with very few races.

White farm kids went to school where I went to school. Cultural sensitivity wasn't an issue because we encountered few cultures, except in the local newspaper. The news rarely celebrated First Nations ceremonies, focusing, rather, on the bands' tragic events. This became my understanding of First Nations life.

I do remember Dad taking us to a rodeo one year hosted by one of the nearby bands. I recall standing on the fence boards watching the horses and riders. A rodeo clown chased a pet skunk, caught it and then threw it up into the grandstand of people. Everyone gasped and ducked. A stuffed skunk landed on one of the bleachers, to the delight of my twelve-year-old self and the rest of the crowd.

Of course, the annual Calgary Stampede festivities include traditional First Nations dancers and I love the ornate costumes: beaded skirts and fancy head dresses of colourful feathers. Something about the dance and chant both haunt and mesmerize me. The reverberating voices stir my soul with equal measures of grief and remembering.

I turned to each of the four directions, offering blessings and feeling each element present in the circle with me. Then I sat for a long time in the September sun. September has always been my favourite month. That shade of blue doesn't exist in any other month's sky. I smelled the dried grasses and decomposing leaves. Though at its lowest point, the creek still provided the faint trickle of movement as it snaked along the coulee floor.

I felt a part of something in nature. I felt no need to be important. Like all of its inhabitants: cricket, magpie, tree, caterpillar, wood lily, coyote and deer, my surroundings welcomed me. Like the teepee ring, we lived in circle together. No one above or below the other.

The elder woman's gift of vision had taken me a long

way since our first meeting atop the hill with the old fence and the scarred earth. Yet, I had not left my home province. That was about to change.

BROKEN barbed wire
  Land fenced off, people fenced out
  Gateway to healing

PART II

STUDIES ABROAD

14

CALIFORNIA CATERING

I packed for California. I was nervous about leaving the kids and Steve on their own, but my cousin was getting married on a mountain top and I'd never gone on a trip just Mom and me. The timing felt right. Amid exploration with my neighbourhood land, I felt an invitation to continue my education abroad.

Anna dropped by for a visit before I left. She brought me something on loan: Fernando's book, *Eagle's Country, The Way of the New Olmecs.* I emailed Fernando to thank him for the previous week's walk and for taking time for me. I mentioned I had a copy of his book and intended to read it on the flight to San Francisco. My education with the land continued as I headed South, destination: Trinity Mountain Range, my fall text book tucked safely into my carry-on.

Cup of water and standard bag of airplane snacks on my tray, I pulled out *Eagle's Country* and settled into my seat. Fernando wrote about Sacred Guardians of the land and special places, and the trees who "...*are the telephones that we can use to communicate with the Great Spirit and all its creatures.*" I marked the page and rested my head back against the seat to contemplate Sacred Guardians of the land. I drifted to sleep.

The last time I was in California with Mom, we had driven down from Alberta. My sister and I rode in the back-seat while Mom and Nan (my grandmother) took turns driving. We headed for Nan's winter rental place in Phoenix, with a side trip to Disneyland.

Ages eight and ten, my sister and I soon bored of the three-day road trip. In the backseat on the floor was a large white paper bag, probably the container of our breakfast or Burnt Almond snack bars. My sister tore off a corner of the bag and wadded it up into a ball. She looked at me and then tossed it into Nan's white hair. I snorted.

Mom sat directly in front of me, her perfectly-coiffed shoulder-length hair poised to collect the paper balls. I tore a corner and pitched it into Mom's hair: white paper against brown curls. We had a lot of time on our hands. We deco-rated the two of them like Christmas trees.

When we all got out of the car for lunch, some of the balls fell but many held strong. My sister and I came clean when Mom demanded to know what we were nearly peeing ourselves over. Knowing Mom, we probably got a raised eyebrow and a stern look. Nan most likely gave a "You girls!"

There was no GPS in the early eighties, no Google Maps to consult, and later that day, we somehow found our way into L.A.'s dodgiest neighbourhood. Mom pulled into a gas station that didn't appear to be serving any gas. Groups of men leaned against the old building and hung out near the taped-off pumps. An intimidating man wearing brass knuckles left his group, crossed the lot and approached Mom's window. From the backseat, my young self sensed both Mom's and Nan's concern. My sister and I sank into the seat.

The sound of the brass knuckles pinged off the glass as he rapped on the window. Mom rolled it down an inch.

"You ladies are in the wrong part of town. You need to leave."

He gave us directions to quickly get back on the freeway. Despite my age, I could tell that this fellow was looking out for us. Things could have gone sideways that day, but a guardian of a different kind had appeared to help us back on our path.

"We are now descending into San Francisco." The Captain's voice woke me. I put my seatback in the standard upright position. We landed safely at our destination. Mom and I hurried to our rental car to get out of San Fran before rush hour.

We hadn't eaten since before our flight but decided to find something en route to Chico, our overnight stop halfway between San Fran and Trinity Mountain Range. The freeway didn't lend itself to roadside cafés or quick and easy meal stops. I didn't fancy a greasy spoon, but we needed something in our stomachs and definitely required water. I had never driven in this part of the state and found myself in unfamiliar territory, reliant upon a little intuition and hope for the best.

We saw nothing from the freeway. We needed to pick an off-ramp and take our chances. I chose one and pulled off onto a side road, no idea how long a detour our search for food would entail. As we rounded a corner in the road, we found ourselves in the middle of orchards loaded with peaches: a colourful contrast to the endless grey freeway of concrete rails, and road signs.

We followed the orchard road, delighted by the loaded fruit trees, and emerged on the main street of a small town. The old buildings wore fresh face-lifts and we cruised along the wide street enjoying the quaint, flower-framed façades.

Old brick businesses gave way to white-fenced historical homes. I love verandas. I always wanted a big front porch to sit on and enjoy iced tea in the summer. There weren't many of those back home. Several spots appealed to us for food: surprising, we thought, for such a small town.

I circled the end of the street so Mom and I could enjoy the parade of Victorian-style three-story homes that had most likely housed the town mayor and founding families. Soft pinks and blues washed over exterior walls. Decorative archways framed generous verandas and turrets topped rooflines like California crowns.

We headed back up main street to the restaurant boasting home-made pie. Surrounded by orchards, the prospect of fresh fruit pie placed them ahead of the other diners and coffee shops. I parked on a wide side street lined with hanging baskets of flowers.

"What a beautiful town," I exclaimed as we got out of the car. The California heat bathed my body as I stretched my back.

In the restaurant we checked out the extensive menu and ordered a couple sandwiches, cookies, bottles of water, and, of course, pie to go. I had expected little from our first stop: a dingy diner perhaps, or a greasy gas station. California welcomed us with open arms, gently nudging us toward our destination, showing us her best along the way.

I settled back into the driver's seat of the car as I settled into the thought that perhaps I wasn't the driver anymore. Maybe Fernando's guardian theory was right. Enjoying my sandwich and the winding orchard road back to the freeway, I put myself and my trip in the hands of our guardian tour guides. I was now on California time. And land.

HOURS LATER, we once again left the freeway as we followed the map to Chico. I had never heard of the city before our trip-planning, but it seemed the most convenient place to overnight between San Fran and our destination. Well, there were more convenient places, but I preferred a place with services and a hotel above a two-star rating.

Mom and I immediately fell in love with Chico. Well-worth the detour from the freeway, our quaint boutique hotel, surrounded by shops, felt luxurious. It appeared Chico also boasted a five-star fitness facility that beckoned me. I phoned over to check the possibility of treating Mom to a pedicure while I hit the gym. Of course they could get us in, because that kind of convenience seemed to be par for the course on our trip. I was beginning to like letting go of the details and accepting that everything would flow smoothly.

"Could we walk from our hotel?" I asked the woman on the other end of the phone. "How far would it be?"

"Oh, about a mile or so up the road," she replied.

We left the hotel and strolled past the art and antique shops, making a note to return in the morning for more than a peek in the windows. We wandered into Bidwell Park. Immense evergreens and towering valley oak trees took our breath away. *Great guardians indeed*. Even the great trees of the Canadian Rocky Mountains dwarfed in comparison to these southern cousins.

Our scenic walk meandered through this inner-city sanctuary until it led us to the most fantastic and unusual place. Right in the middle of the creek was an outdoor swimming pool. An old-fashioned swimming-hole. But this was more than a dip in the creek. This pool had concrete walls and bottom and a ladder to enter, yet the creek flowed straight through.

Kids and adults alike cannonballed off the edges and into the tree-shaded outdoor pool. *What a spectacular feature in a city park. What a wonderful place!* Familiar with the main attractions of California – San Francisco, Los Angeles, Disneyland, Orange County, the Pacific Coast highway – I realized the whole state offered charm and magic. I was falling more and more in love with this land.

"They have skunks in this park?" I asked Mom, who obviously had no more intel on that question than I. "I keep smelling skunk."

"I know," Mom agreed. "Me too."

"Wait a minute," I stopped and faced her with a mixed look of stupidity and insight. "That's not skunk. That's pot." Chico was famous for its University, and Bidwell Park seemed a popular hangout. Still, the odd pockets of putrid perfume did not detract from the scenery.

Character homes filled tree-lined streets and lush, floral gardens appeared to be the norm. We walked on and on, making our way as scenic as possible. There was no rush in our step. Until we hit an intersection and the landscape changed.

A gas station on every corner, great green gave way to grey concrete once more. We had underestimated the walk time to reach the spa and found ourselves in a questionable part of town. I felt certain we were close to our destination, and the local crows confirmed it as they guided us from tree to tree along the road. But as the sky grew darker, so did the neighbourhood. We decided to duck into a convenience store for directions.

"It's just a mile up the road," assured the clerk. *Sure it is.*

We hurried our pace as we passed staring strangers who

began to look stranger and stranger, our feet sore from the distance of our walk, but Mom's feet were in for a pedicure and mine a swim. We arrived at the giant gym/spa facility on a main road in a district far-removed from the quaint shops and restaurants back at our hotel. We agreed to return via cab.

Mom headed to her pedicure room and I bought a bottle of water and hit the gym. I wandered the weight room floor amidst a sea of the latest equipment. The weight room once called me every day during my previous life as a personal trainer, pulling me in for intense sessions of stress-release, empowerment, and escape from frustration and life. Most clients I trained had difficulty getting themselves into a gym; I had difficulty getting myself out of one. I loved my weight training.

Life in the gym changed after my spinal injury. Just before Steve and I married, herniated discs combined with degeneration, stenosis and additional wear and tear on my spine forced me from my passion and purpose as a personal trainer. My recent year in yoga had helped resolve much of the pain and limited range of motion. In fact, it was incredible how much I had healed during that year. But every time I saw perfectly defined pecks or dramatically shaped delts, I secretly longed for my previous muscular frame.

I jumped on a fancy new seated rowing machine in one area, awaiting the fondly-remembered rush that came from pulling the weight. I tried out leg machines in another section of the facility. Nothing. Since my year in yoga, the gym no longer spoke to me. Ancient practices now commanded my ear.

Sitting in an air-conditioned facility on a balmy, California evening certainly had nothing to say either. I felt restless. I grabbed a complimentary towel and headed for the change rooms, hoping the outdoor pool had something more interesting to offer. Good thing I had packed my suit.

I exited the change room to the outdoor pool. A few families visited in hot tubs nearest the doors. I smiled and continued past to the rows of white deck chairs, moving away from the chatter of children.

My jaw dropped at the size and beauty of the pool. It must have had twelve swim lanes, plus a corner pool with waterfall and rock feature. Outdoor pools in the Rocky Mountains were simple and closed for more than half the year. I felt as if I'd stumbled onto an oasis. Golden lights adorned palm trees that moved gently in the breeze against the night sky.

Two men occupied lanes in the pool and a woman lounged in a deck chair watching one of them. I tossed my towel on a chair and dipped a toe into the water, awaiting a bite from the chill. I felt nothing. I lowered myself until the water reached my knees, still nothing. I pushed off the wall. My body merged with water: our temperatures a perfect match. I didn't know where the liquid left, and I began.

The night air kissed my face as California caressed my hair. I swam from starlight to palm light as I completed each length of my private lane. The golden-lit fronds swaying in the breeze seduced me on one end of the pool, while I was awe-struck by the stars sparkling above me on the other end. The two men left the pool and only I remained: my private oasis, well worth the walk.

Adrift in water and thought, my past year in yoga floated through my mind. Before that year, I had hated public pools and had been addicted to weight-training. I had pushed through life, forcing, exerting, and exhausting myself: trying to be the perfect mom, wife and trainer.

The year had taught me to breathe and invite flow into

my life, mind and body. I had learned to forgive myself and to be open to great leaps of faith. I was no longer armed with a defensive retort, but with mantra and mudra. I knew the importance of daily practice and gratitude.

The old me would have capitalized on the state-of-the-art gym and have known nothing of the warm breeze, welcoming water and sparkling sky. She would have never let go and let flow, allowing life to lead her by the hand. As I finished my thought, a shooting star burst across the night above me, applauding my discovery and welcoming me to the new lands. I knew I was in good hands.

RELEASE your belly
unclench your jaw, I have you
I'll show you the world

15

HOLY TRINITY

Nothing but highway for miles and miles. We had left the side roads flanked by orchards and the city of Chico behind. We travelled the main road north and I kept an eye out for our exit to Trinity Mountains.

Like a mirage on a long desert journey, out of nowhere a mountain appeared. A pristine and majestic sight emerged on the horizon in front of me. *How did I not see it sooner?* Snow-capped, it stood alone on the landscape. *Mountains this big don't do that. They attach to other mountains and ease into foothills.* I immediately knew I was face-to-face with Mount Shasta.

A wave of energy danced up my legs, traveled the length of my spine and streamed out each strand of my hair. *Shasta.* I had read about this magnificent mountain as a sacred place and vibrated with excitement to be in her presence. Fortunately, she stood directly in front of me, since my gaze had left the highway and locked deeply onto her. I was mesmerized by her magnitude.

"That's our exit," Mom drew my attention to the road

sign. My thrill caught in my throat along with a lump of longing. It was the closest I was to come to Shasta. Perhaps I could tap into her sacred energy from our location atop Trinity.

I left the interstate and headed west. Mom and I had covered much of California by car. Our new road promised a change of scenery as we moved from open arid landscape into the treed and winding roads of the mountains.

Mom held the overhead handle by her window — the one I like to call the "holy shit handle", because you usually only grab it when the driving gets intense, at which time, you're probably also saying "holy shit" — as I snaked back and forth up the winding mountain road. A control-freak when it came to driving I recognized that I liked to be in charge of my journey, and driving kept me from feeling car-sick, except not this time. The switchback cut into the mountainside went on for over an hour, unsettling even the driver's stomach.

We stopped at the only rest spot we could find, our bladders threatening mutiny. A quaint coffee shack offered ice cream, soda, hot dogs, chips and chocolate bars. We took the time to shake off nausea from the winding drive. The smell of sun-baked pine coerced me to continue our journey. We used the facilities and grabbed waters and dark chocolate for the drive.

"How much further is it to Camp Trinity?" I asked

"Oh, it's just a mile up the road," replied the attendant.

Everything in California was only a mile up the road. Clearly, someone needed to agree on the length of a mile in this state. Mom and I didn't get our hopes up for a short journey. After the previous evening's walking tour of Chico, we were on to the *just a mile up the road* gambit.

No rush. We had a fresh supply of chocolate and water. And a stunning California day.

We reached the site, a long-time summer kids' camp. It truly sat atop the mountain. We pulled up alongside a long, narrow, two-story wooden building that looked like the camp's accommodations. We passed a few tents set up beside the gravel lane, in the grass under large old apple trees, heavy with fruit. My aunt popped out from one of the rooms. Mom lowered her window.

"Well, hello," Mom said to my aunt: the second youngest of the four sisters, Mom being the second oldest. "We made it. Where do you want us?"

Apparently, we had the right building and pulled the car up to unload our gear. We hauled our suitcases up an old wooden staircase with peeling paint onto an equally old wooden porch to our room. Mom and I stood in the middle of the upper floor unit.

Rectangular wooden frames lined two of the walls. Topped with skinny mattresses, they appeared to be our beds. A set of sheets sat folded on each mattress. The floor seemed slanted, covered in linoleum, worn and dated from years of teenage feet. A creaky back door led to an even more slanted hallway which I followed to a rustic wash-room. I kept my eye on the spider in the corner above the door while I relieved my bladder from the remaining drive. I washed up and flicked off the light while simultaneously leaping into the hallway, certain the spider would capitalize on the opportunity to ambush me in the dark.

I returned to the room to find Mom spreading linens across one of the mattresses. "That's the great thing about women," she said as she tucked the corners. "We easily make the best of things. This room is just fine."

No complaining, no eye-rolling or looks of disgust as she unpacked the beautiful new dress she had brought for the ceremony and hung it in the old, wooden closet with no doors. I laughed at her sunny disposition about the room that had me still adjusting my own inner temperature to comfortable reconciliation. There was something about that mountain top and the camp that felt like one could toss a blanket on the ground under the stars and be happy.

We wandered downstairs to explore the property and connect with anyone we knew. The main building was like something out of *The Hobbit*. Several immense trees grew out of the wood-slat cottage as if they were one big tree: an open earthy hand holding the building of old farm-wood and stone in its palm. Mountain stone morphed into steps that wound past the great moss-covered trunk of the tree thumb and into the office entrance.

Two more sturdy trunks grew out of the concrete patio alongside the building. High sprawling branches spread out over the patio like a leafy canopy. The concrete extended to the dining area, filled with picnic tables and protected from the elements by a high, wood-beam roof, slanted for the rain and snow to run off. A low, stone wall enclosed the dining room on one side, open, from the waist up to the view of the property and the late summer breeze.

"Do you girls want to see where the wedding will take place?" My aunt crossed the patio to join us. We headed back up the lane passed the dorm rooms to an outdoor amphitheatre overlooking the camp and mountain range. An arbor of entwined twigs and branches stood in the center. Carved wooden birds suspended from the arch fluttered in the breeze. Rows of seating sculpted into the hillside were separated by stone bases. A family of deer grazed under the large tree behind the seating. All of it set under a blue Cali sky. *What a stunning place to get married.*

Mom chatted with her sister while I wandered over to a small wooden bridge surrounded by tall grasses and marsh water. Monarch butterflies floated around me in the sunlight. I sat on the warm wooden planks, photographing the large, orange beauties. *What a treat for the kids who spent their summers in this sacred place. No wonder my cousin's bride-to-be wanted her wedding where her fondest memories had been.*

Mom and I headed back to our room to get ready for the ceremony. We donned our dresses. I pulled the clip that had tucked my hair neatly away during our day of travel, and let my hair fall into place. I added a little back-combing to tease some volume into my fine hair – a habit firmly etched from my teenage years in the eighties. We returned to the amphitheatre in our heels and dresses.

From my hillside seat I watched the bride and groom join under the wooden birds and archway. The backdrop of meadow, trees and distant mountain tops added to the dreamy feel of the high-altitude wedding. My uncle announced that the couple had been married at City Hall months earlier and that the mountain wedding ceremony was being officiated by a dear friend and colleague of theirs.

I thought the handsome 'Reverend' seemed rather young and casually dressed, with his long hair tied back and his sandals and exposed toes.

"I will be guiding the couple in a four-directions cere-mony," he began. I chuckled. Of course he would. *Of course* I sat on a mountain top under open skies, with Monarch Butterflies, adjacent to one of the most sacred sites in North America, and the ceremony would be conducted in a language I had come to love.

The four directions ceremony had initiated me into my year in yoga and my awakening. It had been shared with me by Leo, the day he cleared my home, and conducted by me at the place of bluebells and bloodshed on the hillside. I closed my eyes and absorbed every word as we turned to face each direction on cue. It was a far cry from the wedding ceremonies we knew growing up, my cousin and I, in our local Presbyterian church.

My thoughts drifted to my wedding with Steve. We may have not known the four-directions ceremony, but we had the open sky as our church roof, the warm ocean breeze and waters to bless us, and an officiant who spoke and sang with Aloha as we danced our first dance as husband and wife, barefoot in the sand to ukulele while turtles looked on. It seemed somehow less about the script and more about the blessings of Nature.

Ceremony complete, we made our way down the lane toward the dining deck at the main building. The modest mess hall was transformed into a celebratory garden party. Tea lights nested in pebbles in glass jars hung above the tables, where white linens and potted green plants looked crisp and fresh under the glowing lanterns. Tiny golden lights adorned the trunks of trees like fireflies around the main building. People took turns posing for photos with the bride and groom between the glowing green giants.

Mom and I grabbed a glass of lemonade and visited on the grass. We looked lovely, not a stretch for Mom as she always looked exquisite. Funny though, considering the room where we prepared ourselves wasn't exactly glamorous. Mom was right, we could easily make the best of things. I felt like she and I were at camp.

Dinners, speeches; the sun began to set yet the California air remained unchanged, providing a blanket of warmth as the darkness emerged. The tallest of trees that provided a roof for our dance floor, sparkled with soft golden lights. I stood in a fairy tale. This particular tale was set to a modern score and I kicked off my heels to dance the night barefoot on the cement under the sparkling branches and distant stars while 90's beats blasted from speakers.

Mom and I called it a night and headed back up the lane in the dark.

"Look," she said. We stopped dead in our tracks.

"I've never seen a sky like this," I said. "Not even at home. So many stars. I didn't know it was possible to see this many from Earth."

I grew up in the country without the city lights to hamper the view at night. We witnessed immense harvest moons and northern lights as kids. I knew the Big Dipper, Orion, and Cassiopeia as close friends, yet I had never, in all my childhood years, seen a sky like this.

Even the years I spent working and living in the Rocky Mountain tourist town of Banff in my mid-twenties, witnessing the hissing, crackling northern lights snaking green and pink across the secluded and distant end of Lake Louise, I had never seen so many stars. Layers upon layers of celestial lights surrounded us as if we stood at the highest point on Earth. We sat on the shoulders of Trinity while she gave us a boost to see more of what the universe offered. And the universe leaned in for a closer look.

Even the sound of tiny creature feet across the old dorm floor that night— a mouse? Lizard? Who knew? — didn't dent the lingering awe of the evening's light show. Sleeping in my yoga pants, in case whatever slowly navigated the linoleum decided to join me in bed, I pulled up my sheet and fell asleep to distant 80's rock, drunken cheers, and the thud of ripe apples falling on the ground from the great old tree out my door.

I SEE you see me
   To know you is to know me
   You must remember

16

STANDING STONES

I woke early in anticipation of quiet time to connect with the land and perhaps the Guardians Fernando spoke of. An early morning walk and meditation might offer insight as to my next steps in life. I headed down to the main building, passing the old canopy tree still wearing last night's jewels. Quiet hung on the air like the lanterns on the great tree. My warm breath danced with the crisp mountain morning. I made my way across the road, unsure which direction to travel. A figure leaned on the fence on the other side of the road. It was my cousin, the groom.

I wasn't the only early explorer. My cousin and his new wife both worked as birders. They caught, tagged and released birds to track their migration and numbers. They shared a love of nature. My cousin's new bride joined us. They were headed for an early morning walk and told me of a trail I could follow that led to a river below. My cousin warned me to be on the lookout for bears.

Of course I had to be on the lookout for bears. Bear energy always seemed to keep me alert and a little afraid when I sought solace and sacred space in nature. On top of wandering around unknown territory, I now also had to keep my guard up for bear. I thanked them, wished them a nice walk and headed to the trail.

Not even twenty feet down the treed path, I stepped over a rather substantial pile of fresh you-know-what. Bear had been there. It appeared he was ahead of me, leading the way, dropping his breadcrumbs along the trail. I stayed alert and moved quietly along the path. I knew the bear was too big for the tree-lined trail and his or her descent would be noisier than mine.

The trail wound down the heavily treed mountainside. My senses expanded in every direction. Cool air cleared my nostrils. A forest Fan Deck of green lit my sight. No paint palette could compare to nature's studio. The sound of my feet treading lightly on the dirt path laid down the tempo of my trek. My heartbeat, drummed on my chest wall, enlivened by nature and elevated by fear. Every cell stood alert to sound, movement or sense of bear energy. The trail gently landed me at a farm.

I stood at the treeline and debated taking the gravel road to my left, which I assumed led to the river. A large garden across the road fostered the biggest sunflowers I had ever seen. The golden maidens watched over the mountain nursery. They must have stood eight feet tall with faces larger than mine. I had intended to go to the river, but another area pulled me to the side. It also occurred to me my furry trail guide had headed to the water for a morning drink.

Many horses stood in a clearing in front of me framed by tall trees. In the center of the clearing was a large standing stone with a flat top. I walked to the stone and placed my hand on its smooth surface. There was a pair of sunglasses on it. Someone else had enjoyed the stony rest stop. I perched myself atop the ample seat and my bum met the cold of the stone.

Sitting on the rock, I saw how the trees surrounded it, not in a grove, but in a single semi-circular line; as if they were in attendance, listening to some great tale told by the stone storyteller. It felt like a place of power and the horses knew it. They stood munching on grass. I knew if the horses were content, no bear was near, and I felt safe in their company. One wandered over and tried to eat the sunglasses. I pulled them from her lips and rubbed her velvety nose.

The horses migrated past the trees and toward the main house in the distance. I remained on the rock as if I sat in council, listening. My cousin and his wife popped out of the trees. I jumped off the rock and pretended to do yoga, folding into triangle pose. Like that was less weird than sitting on the rock in meditation? Clearly, I felt my new normal wasn't quite normal. They turned onto the gravel road, heading for the river, and dropped out of sight. I gave up my trikonasana, I'm not sure I tricked anyone, and settled back into my spot on the rock.

No messages came. No visions appeared. The place felt magical, but I could get no signal. Maybe I didn't speak their language. Perhaps I was trying too hard or was preoccupied with the return of my heightened senses for the bear, now that the horses had moved on. Maybe I expected too much. I stayed anyway, hands in meditative mudra on my knees, eyes closed, soaking up the sacred and silent energy of the place: a reverent guest.

When I emerged at the top of the trail Mom was standing near the main road.

"Come here," I called. "Check this out!" An enormous wooden tree swing overlooked the mountain valley. A great tree effortlessly held the massive wooden seat by one strong, leafy arm. We sat on the bench. Our feet dangled like toddlers as we swung out over the view in front of us. What a peaceful place, a nourishing place. I thought I would be disappointed to not receive a vision or have the land tell me its story, but I felt deeply at peace. I felt as if I didn't need a purpose in this place. To *be* in this place was purpose enough.

THINK WE SAID NOTHING?
> *We spoke volumes through silence*
> *showing you the way*

17

GRACE EXPOSED

I stepped outside to see my sixty-four-year-old mother head-to-head with a naked penis, making me rethink my decision to book this resort. We had said our good-byes to Trinity Mountain Range that morning and made our way to our next stop before heading back home to Canada. My brief check-in at the front office left Mom vulnerable in the rental vehicle. Seated in the car, she was penis-level for the nude resort passer-by. I knew Harbin had a clothing-optional policy at the hot springs but didn't realize it spilled out over the entire property on the busy weekends.

I took a deep breath, opened the driver-side door and got back in the car. Mom commented on the nudity, and I started to defend, then decided to let it go. We parked the car in the main lot where a baggage cart operator greeted us and offered us a ride. He pulled up in front of the quaint cottage I had reserved weeks earlier, the only one with a claw-footed tub which I selected especially for Mom to enjoy after our rustic lodgings at the mountain-top wedding.

A blanket of lawn spread out from the road to our

colourful character cottage. It was a storybook scene except for the multitude of living lawn ornaments. It would have to be an x-rated storybook: naked bodies strewn across the entire lawn provided a delicate obstacle course to navigate, especially with suitcases in hand. Mom and I kept our eyes on the front door of the cottage and made our way, polite Canadians, "Excuse me. Pardon me. Excuse us please."

Inside, the cottage smelled of rose geranium. A quilt-covered queen bed sat in the middle of the room. The bathroom glowed with natural light. Three walls with large windows draped with lace sheers brightened the room. Mom closed the door to use the toilet, only to open it again quickly.

"I can't use the toilet," she said. "There are people all over the lawn and they can see me."

"They're all naked, Mom," I replied. "I'm pretty sure the last thing they are interested in is you peeing."

I didn't know where else to go with that. An exercise on exposure and comfort levels seemed at hand, only we were clothed yet appeared the most vulnerable on the resort. Thank goodness the claw-foot tub was strangely located in the bedroom and not on display in the bathroom. We unpacked a few items and set out to explore.

We made our way once again past the naked nymphs and gnomes. As I allowed myself eye contact, I noticed the lawn loungers consisted of families, small kids, seniors, and singles; all appeared comfortable, content, and utterly relaxed. The scene, and my feelings about it, reminded me of the South of France and one of my first experiences with public nudity, well, topless-ness anyway.

When nudity is the norm discomfort ceases to exist. When clothing-optional occurs solely in the privacy of your own home, as it did where Mom and I grew up, discomfort tends to be acute. As I saw the faces of the kids happily playing on the lawn, and the return smile of the parents as they met my gaze, I briefly forgot about the clothes or lack thereof. I saw people enjoying a warm weekend day.

Thankfully two large canvas tents set up near our cottage: shopping. One tent boasted of hand-dyed silk tops and dresses, scarves, and yoga wear. The other burst with clothing from India, Indonesia, and other exotic origins. Colourful tunics, dresses, pants, sweaters, blankets, and magnificent crystal and gem jewelry spilled off of racks and out of display boxes. Mom and I delighted in the reprieve of the unexpected bazaar. Undecided between the emerald green or ruby red silk camisoles, Mom wanted to try them on but not without a change room.

"Um, Mom, you know everyone around you is naked, right?" I teased her. The warm boutique lady didn't miss a beat. She plucked a large silk scarf from a rack and held it up as a glamorous curtain for Mom. Mom expressed her appreciation to the woman, and they chatted while she changed clothes.

As I witnessed the exchange, I learned something. Until that moment I had been thinking about how I should feel more comfortable around the nudity, accept the conditions around me, and even consider acting more like the regulars. What I learned in that moment, watching Mom's graceful exchange, was that when in Rome, you don't always have to do as the Romans do.

We may have stuck out like sore thumbs, but there was nothing sore about us. The regulars were comfortable in their skin and we were comfortable in our clothes. Mom and I each bought a silk cami and chose a gemstone pendant and chain: me, a teardrop moonstone, and Mom, a rose quartz heart. I thought they suited us brilliantly. Mom's grace, beauty, strength, and love pulsed from the rose-coloured heart, and my affinity for magic, otherworldly experiences, reflection and luminescence dripped from the moonstone.

We lined up for dinner: a long line but several resort-goers had mentioned how amazing the food was in the restaurant. The comforting aroma wafting across the large room filled with fully-clothed patrons promised us the food was worth the wait. We stood in queue near the back of the room and next to a table with one heavier-set, older gentleman sporting a long grey beard. He made a comment, as we were in such proximity to his dining it was hard to ignore one another, and Mom responded. I would have left it there and fixed my gaze firmly to the front of the line to signal that our communication had ended. Mom continued the exchange.

It turned out he was a teacher of rune stones. That got my attention. I swivelled my stance into a more open posture and listened intently, taking mental notes. Mom was her social self, chatting freely with him. Some say the politeness is a Canadian thing. I wrongfully felt the polite amusing of someone else's conversation, whether you were interested or not, was a family trait I wanted to free myself of. I wanted to choose only in that which I was truly interested, and speak my mind, seeing the social humouring of the man that my Mom, and I, permitted and perpetuated, as some form of weakness.

What I came to understand was that behaviour, that social mask, was less of a mask and far more of a grace. A grace that was gifted to us from my grandmother, Mom's Mom, and I'm sure her grandmother, and hers, and most women in our lines. It's what came naturally to us and I knew how powerful it was in helping others feel comfortable, welcomed and included, and opened the door to interesting conversations and connections. It appeared I had more interest in the story of land than the story of those who lived upon it.

The natural ability we had to converse politely and warmly was indeed a gift, and I had tried to deny it as I found my more masculine way in the world, what I thought was my stronger, more independent self. Later, that grace was something I believed I needed to seek and find, forgetting it was part of my heritage, part of my upbringing, and part of my feminine self.

In my pursuit of strength, I had denied my natural grace. In my years of proving I was as good as any man, I had forgotten how great it was to be a woman. I let myself believe that grace meant weakness and would leave me vulnerable and as naked as the resort's weekend guests. The interesting part was that the guests looked anything but vulnerable. In fact, they looked joyful, happy, and at ease: where they were, as they were.

JUDGMENT, labels, views
  Do you use your eyes to see?
  Maybe use your heart

18

CLEARING FEAR

Back home, I lay face-up on Sophie's reiki table. My stomach had been giving me trouble: bloating, pain, sluggish. She ran her hands above me, sensing any blockages. She stopped at my midsection.

"You've been doing more clearing of the land, haven't you?" she asked.

"Yes," I replied. "I'm still walking around my neighbourhood. There is one section of trees in a valley that feels too dense and dark. I want to go in there, but it feels like a place I need to go with others. It freaks me out. I don't know what happened there."

"You're picking up things from the land," she said. "You need to find a way to clear without moving it through your body. It's getting stuck."

I didn't want to be afraid to walk the land. I didn't want to start worrying about what I was picking up. Was I picking stuff up? What stuff? Was that even possible?

I know that one plus one equals two. I don't even give the answer three a second thought. I know three's not true. The issue with spiritual exploration is that it was relatively new to me. I didn't know what was true. And when I don't know something, fear has a natural way of becoming my first line of defense.

We fear what we don't know. But sometimes we have to stop being afraid in order to know something. I loved walking the land. I could stick to my desire to not pick up stuff from the land, but if that wasn't true, if that really wasn't the case and I could indeed attract unwanted energy from my walks, then I needed to know more about this subtle work. I needed clarity from the most experienced walker I knew. I emailed Fernando.

WE WALKED the paved path along the river. This time we didn't travel in silence. I think Fernando could tell my mind was heavy with concern.

"Is it possible to pick up stuff we clear from the land?" I asked, pulling my jacket around me to block the windchill.

Fernando knew my concern. "As long as you walk with a clear mind, open heart and no fear," he replied, "you could walk with Hitler himself and nothing will happen to you."

His answer made perfect sense to me. Just as feelings of love tend to attract and promote further feelings of compassion, forgiveness, and kindness, feelings of fear tend to attract and engage feelings of anger, hostility, and paranoia. I wouldn't do reiki on someone while I was in a state of fear or anger. I use love and compassion, joy and clarity to remove blockages. Walking the land required the same loving care as working with a client or family member. You clear land energy as one would clear their own: removing blockages as one might find in TCM and Qigong, along the meridians in the earth.

"Would you come to my home studio and give an informal talk to my friends and clients?" I asked.

Fernando obliged. The following week he and his wife, Carmen, came to share their stories with a small group in my home studio. Three of us were so drawn by Fernando's work that we soon joined him in his home for meditation. We wanted to continue the work, the land-clearing he had done so many years in Mexico, in our own city.

OUR GROUP of five sat around Fernando and Carmen's coffee table, candles flickered and danced on the table between us.

"Stephanie," said Fernando, "since you have gathered this family, would you like to lead the meditation?"

I guided the group into our collective meditative journey to discover where in our city we would begin our work of clearing. Once my mind and body relaxed, images darted across my mindscape and I followed their story.

Once complete, I opened my eyes to see where everyone else in the group was in their process. Fernando sat with his eyes open. Then Carmen opened hers. Anna was next. My other friend struggled, eyes closed, trying to stay in meditation. I waited patiently for Fernando to conclude the process. He said nothing.

I watched her continue to strain behind closed eyes. Her brow furrowed. I began to feel tense myself. *Why doesn't he wrap it up?* After a prolonged and uncomfortable window, I realized I had opened the meditation and it was up to me to close it. *Whoops. Rookie mistake.* Heat rushed my face. I quickly concluded the process and we began to share our individual meditative insights, looking for common threads.

In a familiarly fascinating way, each person's visions,

once collectively revealed, led us to the places to walk in Calgary to begin our work. It felt ordained. And frightening.

We were not ready to take up the work after all. As much as we shared a deep desire to heal our communities and deepen our spiritual learning, 3a.m. silent walking through the downtown streets seemed a tall order for women with small children at home. A sense of desire became a sense of duty. And that duty felt heavy. Too heavy for me.

The group simply moved apart as silently as the sacred walks. There was no mention of the work or call to action by any of its members. It wasn't that I didn't want to join Fernando in continuing his work; it was that the call wasn't strong enough to pull me into committed action. Not enough to leave my family in the wee hours and walk the streets of Calgary.

I was honoured to know Fernando, of his work and his story. There was simply no wave for me to ride that pulled me into practice. Not like when I experienced my year in yoga. There was a force behind that call. One that made it easy, well not easy, but necessary and compelling enough to pull me from my family and commit to a year of daily practice. I rode the wave and the wave took me places. I couldn't wait to see where it would take me next.

I didn't feel that force for the early morning walking ritual. Once again, I had been looking for a purpose — a noble, sacred purpose — but this was not mine. This was not my call.

MY PATH IS NOT yours
  My knowledge, though, I will share
  A wise walking stick

19

A RED ROCK RITE OF PASSAGE

Anna dropped me off at the trailhead to Cathedral Rock. I waved as she pulled out of the parking lot and drove off to Bell Rock. We had decided to spend a few hours in personal exploration: each with her own journey. I walked through the sparse desert trees along the path from the parking lot to the rock's smooth foundation. I stood on the wide base, looking up at the towering rock before me. I remembered Leo's email, sent to me from Vancouver days before my departure.

> *I hope you get to go to cathederal rock in sedona, actually you have to go there alone... there is something wonderful, wonderful about to happen Steph, and the rock will tell you. I will be there in spirit, so will my ancestors... watch for the signs. leo*

I took a deep breath and hoped to hear the rock's guidance but, quite frankly, didn't expect much and felt pissed off at Leo's cryptic instructions. Yet another message that triggered doubt in my abilities to know my intuition and trust it. I understood Leo lived by the guidance of Spirit. He had suffered an accident when he was younger, followed by a supernatural experience that led him to leave life as a University Professor, and to learn to follow ancient traditions and nature's guidance. Even after my visions, my experiences in nature and my meeting Fernando, I still doubted my ability to connect as purely as Leo.

I stood at the wooden sign. *Cathedral Rock* and *Templeton Tr* were carved into the wood with arrows pointing in odd directions as they do when you try to indicate multiple locations from one flat plane. It looked as though Templeton Trail was in the sky. I emptied my mind.

My attention drifted to a path left of the main one, apparently Templeton Trail, and I decided to follow it to what looked like the back of the rock. The trail would take me around the rock, not up the actual climb. Disappointed I would not be reaching the top, I trusted my gut and headed off along the flat base.

I passed another person, confirming the trail I chose was indeed a worn path. It was hard to tell on the smooth red rocks, unlike the hiking trails in the Rockies back home where frequent use wore a path through wild grasses, shrubs and exposed tree roots. You were either on the trail, in the bushes or off the mountainside, unlike the red rocks where you could easily wander off course. My first time in Sedona. I did not know about the cairns that marked the trails to keep hikers on course.

I came to a shaded place on the path. To my left, the trail veered away from the rock's peaks and around a corner that hid its destination from sight. To my right appeared a hidden waterfall. It was dry, but the steep, smooth rock face resembled a giant waterslide. Patterns of red and orange stained the rock where water flowed during the rainy seasons. The slide was several stories tall with large bumps that kept me from seeing the entire chute.

As kids, we travelled to British Columbia each summer for holidays. Mom and Dad often stopped at a popular tourist spot on the highway along the way. It was a tall slide with many humps and bumps: a magic carpet ride. Kids grabbed a sack and climbed the stairs to the top, waited their turn, scooted into their sacks and rode the humps and waves down the slide. I felt like a kid at an outdoor playground as I stared at the dry waterfall. At the top stood twin spires, the crowning glory of Cathedral rock.

With no idea if the waterfall bed was even passable, I headed straight toward it. It was a long way up. I had three hours before Anna would retrieve me at the trailhead. I stopped at the base of the chute and thought about Fernando and his experience with the mountain. I silently acknowledged all who joined me on my pilgrimage: Leo, Fernando, the Guardians. I knew deeply that it was the mountain itself, the imposing red rock and the earth, that extended the invitation and would ensure my safe passage. I accepted her outstretched hand and headed up over the first small hump.

The smooth rock was surprisingly easy to climb. I had assumed with few trees to assist my ascent, the climb would prove challenging. However, I felt like a mountain goat as my hiking shoes strangely adhered to the red rock, even on a steep angle. Over the initial hump I discovered a small pool of water. A shaded puddle on my desert climb stood out like a sore thumb.

I paused, opting to take my time with the tiny pool and crouched beside it. I touched the water and the tiniest water snake started dancing. Like a thin, black string, about three inches long, it swam and writhed in its red rock water bowl.

What a strange creature; and to find something so unique living in a small and fleeting pool of water on the side of the rock. I later researched my little water snake to discover it was a horsehair worm or Gordian worm, from the Gordian knot, named so as they often tie themselves in knots. That sounded familiar. It appeared the tiny pool presented an interesting reflection.

I watched the show for a while and then sized up my next hump — not too bad, a bit steeper than the first. I stepped up onto the sloping wall. No hand holds presented themselves. I needed to learn how to walk with the rock. I headed up and over to find more than a tiny pool. I found a small oasis. A tree sat at the back of the next landing, with tufts of grass and moist red clay beneath.

I paused for a moment, considering the shrubby enclave might conceal larger wrigglers and quick-striking creatures. I kicked a couple small stones into the area and made some noise, deciding it best to sit on the exposed rocks opposite the tree. As I rested, I noticed someone else had made it there before me. Carvings in the damp clay near the base of the tree, and shoe prints nearby, told me I wasn't the first to discover the secret garden.

Perhaps I wasn't as off-trail as I originally thought. Oh well, I didn't need to go rogue to connect to nature. Intrigued by the clay art, I squatted near it to decipher its meaning. A spiral, a heart and letters that appeared incomplete or only of significance to their scribe. I wondered what they came looking for. What was the clay artist seeking? Healing? Love? Connection? All three? Did they ask for something specific? A solution to a problem or a cure for a disease? Did they ask for themselves or for the earth? Did they, too, seek their place on the planet?

I considered staying at the oasis, taking the symbols, the tree, and the hideaway as a sign of a sacred place. Perhaps I should stop seeking and simply be happy to remain at this place, in meditation and contentment with what is. I looked up at the spires: erect, red giants: alien elders atop the rock. I saw the sun on the ridge above and it looked as though I could easily walk along it to the top if I just got over the next hump.

The back wall was steep, more so than the previous waterfall steps. The height of it proved difficult for me to surmount. I could not step up that high and I couldn't walk up it as it was nearly a ninety-degree angle. I could get my hands on top of it but it wasn't high enough for a true chin-up, and too high for a press-up. I knew I had the upper body strength to get myself up there if I could only negotiate the strange height.

Brute strength would not serve me. I needed to consider another way. I placed my hands atop the ledge and one foot on the wall. Thank the Goddess for yoga. I shifted my weight and felt my way into a position that supported me against the smooth, cool rock. I leaned in, shifted again and was able to pull myself up with my arms, clearing the hump.

I stood looking over all the ground I had covered and the height I had climbed, the base of the rock, the tiny pool with the wee water snake and the oasis of spiral and heart. I looked at the wall I surmounted and hoped there was another way down because scaling that steep hump made it impossible to go back. I could not descend that way without injury. The decision to take that next step had closed the door behind me. I looked up at the sun's light on the ridge and the towering spires and continued my journey.

I walked toward the back of the next step, assuming it would open up to lead me to the top. I rounded a gentle corner to find the steepest wall yet, insurmountable. Not at all as I had thought. *Damn.* I sat down on a rocky seat against the opposite wall of the chute and pulled my journal and pen from my shorts pocket.

I had made a mistake. I pushed ahead under an assumption and I was wrong. I took a gamble. I thought the next step would be the one that took me to my higher purpose, the top of the rock and the coveted spire elders. In that moment I understood my pattern and wrote in my journal.

Pushing through - higher, further - to get to the top, reach the bar, has been my method for as long as I can remember. Where is the top? Is it physical, mental, emotional? Is it within me or without? I wondered if I could have been happy staying at the oasis below. I looked up at the spires, sadly out of reach, and contemplated my predicament.

I had not seen another person since the main trail. I could not go back the way I came up. The rock brought me to the concealed dry waterfall. There had to be a way to continue or return. Then something terrible happened.

My stomach started to churn. I had no idea how long I'd been climbing but suddenly felt the heat of the desert gaining strength. My stomach was not a fan of heat, particularly dry heat coupled with the heat of exertion. I had to go to the bathroom. BAD.

There was no holding it and it mortified me to think I would be forced to defecate on the red rocks. All my holding within, keeping things inside and dealing with them in discreet and proper ways, came to the surface as my body gave me no options in the matter. Nature called and I had to answer.

I shuddered to think of anyone crapping on a state park

and the pristine red rocks, but my stomach forced my hand. *Why now?* At any other point I could have made it back to the trail. Why when I was stuck on this ledge? Indeed, stuck between a rock and a hard place, my bowels gave me the thirty-second warning and then they were taking over.

The waterfall step offered no cover, no shrubbery, no leaves, nothing. Thankfully no hikers or tourists either. I pulled several pages from my journal, happy that at least the paper was hand-made and eco-friendly. Somehow in my mind that lessened my impact.

I crouched along the far wall, around the gentle rock corner and did my business, apologizing to the rock. I returned to my previous seat along the opposite wall shaking my head at my predicament but feeling immense relief from relieving myself. A calm washed over me as I thought of Fernando's book and his account of his experience with the mountain. I trusted all would be well and relaxed into my rocky seat, sun on my face, head against the wall behind me.

The rock wall suddenly looked different than before. I saw a clear path to the ledge above. *That's not possible. Where did that come from?* I had checked the entire area. There was no way to proceed.

I got up and headed to the wall. Sure enough, there was a thin ledge concealed behind some higher shrubs that looked like it might support me. I squeezed behind the rock wall and stepped up onto the ledge. Holding onto the wall, I shimmied my way along the steep rock, looking down to where the cove had provided a bathroom. It seemed I had to dump all my shit in order to continue my journey.

I crept along the ledge, grasping onto shrub and root handles, pulling myself firmly to the rock wall and not looking down. The sheer discovery of an exit, one that allowed me to continue to move forward, re-energized me and kept my fear of heights at bay.

I paused and pulled my cell phone from my pocket with one hand, gripping loose shrubs firmly with the other. I stood, perched on a tiny ledge, overlooking the path I'd journeyed, intoxicated by how far I'd climbed. It was a breathtaking view and I felt immensely grateful and happy, an empowered explorer. I took a couple pictures before fear gave me a good, swift reminder that I was precariously perched on the side of the wall and a fall could mean the end of more than this journey.

I tucked my phone back into my pocket and continued along the ledge until I found smoother and higher ground. I emerged onto a vast plane of rock. I wandered about the hilltop, pulled in one direction and another, feeling woozy. Was it the effect of the vortex that people and books referenced or had I climbed high enough for altitude to become a factor. My head spun and I needed to breathe deeper.

I followed the smooth terrain as it lured me away from the spires. I sat on the edge of a large rocky mound. Pockets of clear crystals sparkled from the warm, red surface. I scratched at one with my fingernails. They were solidly embedded in the rock, impossible to dislodge, a dazzling desert treasure. The magnificent jeweled rocks emerged from the desert floor like great aliens in a foreign land. To see the crystal pockets lit by the sun increased the otherworldly effect.

I was torn in two directions. I wanted to continue exploring the red plains, which were effortless to move about on and dropped gently onto level after level of rock. I felt certain I could make my way down, easily following the amiable terrain. But over my shoulder, the tall spires beckoned. I had come all this way, I needed to reach the top. I abandoned my blissful, sunny state on the flat rock to continue climbing in the shadow of the spires.

I headed toward the towers that stood atop the mountain like a great council gathering. I reached the end of the manageable terrain and stood at the opening between the two main figures of the council. Rocky shale covered my path to the top, and a steep one at that. I decided to brave it since sparse trees and desert shrubs provided a buffer between me and a red rock fall, should I slip and slide down the shale.

The final ascent felt familiar, like the mountain-tumbled path of the upper Rockies. Once you clear the tree line, it is just you, the mountain, and the weather. Only it wasn't just me and the mountain. It was me and a gathering of spires at the top. I took the final step in my climb to find the end of the road.

I stood, legs shaking from the climb, cradled between two red rock figures reaching skyward. The cradle proved only five or six feet long and equally wide. *I reached the top.* I took in the view from where I'd come and the one from the back side of the rock, which appeared non-negotiable as a route of continuation. Although I considered it as the next challenge, I dismissed it and decided I had accomplished enough for one day.

I pulled my phone from my pocket and recorded video of the view and the cradle. My breathless commentary was proof of the work I had done along the way to the peak. I put my phone away and stood between the spires, uncomfortable by the uneven terrain on which I perched. I stood on shaky ground, or more accurately, shaky legs. I'm certain the ground was more than stable.

I quickly sat to appease my fear of heights. I gazed at the view from my perch, face to face with the highest points of the red rocks in the distance. I felt like a giant, one among the alien council. I sat with sky and mountain peaks, and the realm of the Gods. I felt otherworldly.

Words came on the breeze. *Trust. Faith. Guidance. Seek silence and guidance is there. Trust it. Follow it.* I sat, listening for guidance, seeking a message and the certainty to know I heard and understood it correctly.

Insights abound in the journey, the destination is the gravy. With that knowing, I got up to leave but was instead pulled to lay down on my back and take my gaze skyward between the two red rock fingers.

They towered above me like gates between worlds. The blue sky glowed background to the rusty red. Two eagles soared above me in circles on the thermals, figure-eights above the red rocks. A giant bug zoomed over me, flying between the spires. *What the hell was that?* I'd never seen such a large flying insect.

I felt giddy with joy — almost drunk — as I lay on my back. I pulled out my phone once more and took pictures of myself laying in my red rock cradle, staring up at great giants, watched over by eagles. I felt goofy and happy. A mask of light on my face, around my eyes, appeared in the photo.

The cool red rocks were hard yet comfortable as their shapes cradled the contours of my body. A tiny winged creature landed on the page of my journal as I jotted down my experience. I laughed, thinking the faeries were delighted my inner child had returned to play atop the red rocks. I felt lit from within.

I could have stayed in my rocky cradle for hours, staring up at my new friends. The sun shifted position during my time in the cradle and moved around to warm me. I lingered, enjoying the heat on my face. And like a child I forgot about time.

TIME SPENT COMPLAINING
struggle against the mountain
Appreciate her

20

WHAT GOES UP

I slid down the shale, partly on my bum. I didn't have time to descend over the smooth, rocky plain that had lured me on the climb. I wasn't certain it would lead me back to the trailhead, although my gut said most likely yes. But it may have taken a while to navigate and I needed to meet Anna.

I found a worn trail and followed it in the opposite direction, the direction of the parking lot on the other side of the rock. It led to a narrow ridge with a breath-taking view. Two people stood on the ridge taking pictures. I inhaled the view but saw no apparent route down. In fact, it seemed more treacherous than the one I took up. I asked the couple, "How do you get down from here?"

They looked at me strangely, obviously wondering how I got up, if not the tourist trail. "You follow the cairns and the path right there," they replied, pointing to a shale trail I had not seen. I headed down the trail. It connected to a wider path. Indeed, there were cairns at every turn. I hadn't noticed them nor knew of their purpose. No wonder the couple had looked at me strangely.

Tourists became plenty and the path crowded. I often stepped off it, waiting for others to pass before I continued with my descent. The chatter and energy of others shocked me. I realized how isolated I had been for those glorious three hours. I trotted down the trail, light on my feet and agile on the terrain as it carried me quickly and confidently down the rock side. I laughed at the fact that only a short while earlier I was reassuring myself the rock would show me a way down.

Then I heard my name. I stopped and looked below over the smooth shelves of the lower rock and saw Anna. I climbed down to where she stood, and we exchanged hugs of greetings. We briefly acknowledged our respective sacred times and their powerful impact, then we got to the good stuff: taking photos of ourselves on the red rock with the desert trees. I smiled into the camera and up at the Guardian that had taken excellent care of me.

Famished after our experiences with the red rocks, Anna and I headed for town. We happened upon a small restaurant on the main road. The ChocolaTree seemed the perfect lunch spot for two lovers of chocolate. Vegetarian wraps and cold coconut water with herbal elixirs: we'd found heaven.

We sat at a nearby table. I picked up the deck of angel cards that occupied the space where salt and pepper were usually found. I looked at Anna. We at once scanned the room to discover decks of angel or tarot cards on every table. Giant, earthy-coloured lingams separated the tables from the merchandise: shelves of crystals, cards, statues and art.

I walked up to the counter to order, passing a coffee table and comfy chairs nestled behind the lingam wall. I eavesdropped on the occupants of this cozy nook. "You will most definitely find love." A woman provided a card-reading for a client.

At the counter stood a display bursting with chocolates. Anna and I were in awe of the paradise we had discovered. Fresh, delicious, healthy food and herbal elixirs satisfied my thirst like no amount of water could have done. Chocolates presented in as many flavours as I could conjure in my imagination, and to top it off, all the New Age fun we could handle.

Conversations of chakras and meditation and vortices encircled us. We stared at each other, mouths and eyes wide. We couldn't believe our circumstances. It was as if we had gone down the rabbit hole and emerged in Sedona. We didn't need to lower our voices to share our morning's hiking experiences. Our words were as liberated as our spirits in that moment.

We left the ChocolaTree with bags of dark chocolate delights and promptly discovered an appealing store down the street. The large shop boasted at least one hundred varieties of divination cards, books, incense, candles, chakra banners, Buddha statues, dream catchers, crystals, journals, spiritual jewelry, carved masks, tuning forks, and a myriad of mystical merchandise.

Upon entering, I felt enticed by the buffet of delectable spiritual morsels. As I flipped through books, sampled card packs, and held crystals, I began to feel overwhelmed. Pressure built inside my head and gut and I needed to use their washroom. Although initially delighted by the selection, I felt confused by the variety and frustrated at my desire to find items that would help lead me to my purpose.

Maybe just the right crystal or a particular journal provided the clarity I needed to see it. In my eagerness to discover the next clue on my path, certain it could be found somewhere in the store and quickly forgetting my experience with Cathedral Rock that morning, I took my selection to the counter. My purchases included a couple crystals, a deck of cards, and several books. Books? Had I completely forgotten I travelled by plane with one small, neatly packed carry-on? Did it slip my mind that books were heavy and could be found or ordered just about anywhere?

I loved a fresh, new book with an appealing cover that said, "Come see what's inside. I have the answers. I'll tell you a story you won't forget." A stack of books next to my bed stood ready for me to leaf through at my whim. I loved to pick up a book and ask, "What do I need to know today?" And then flip to any page that called me.

I hauled my heavy purchases around, hoping they contained treasure and my purpose on their pages somewhere. I was willing to carry the burden I thought might reveal my next step. By the time I would make my return trip home, hauling my baggage through two airports, I would be cursing my choice as my shoulder strained under the weight, and willing to ditch my so-called treasure.

Anna and I both felt taxed by the brief shopping excursion. It struck me that the three hours spent scaling a dry waterfall recharged me yet one hour in a store drained me. Sunset loomed on our day. We headed for a popular spot to watch it drop.

Due to the late hour, we entered the park at no charge. We parked our rental car and made our way on foot between great old trees to a green space. I looked up at the red rock tower in the distance. Lit by the setting sun, it was the main attraction for the park. It was Cathedral Rock from the other side. I had begun my day looking up at those spires on fire in the bright morning sun. I completed my first day in Sedona looking up at the rock council once more, this time glowing orange embers in the evening rays.

I followed Anna through a path in the trees near the

creek. She seemed to know where she was going. The air now cooled my skin, goosebumps rising to meet it. We passed people hugging trees, meditating at the bases of trees, and even a couple seated on large rocks across the creek, eyes closed, legs crossed: human meditative statues for all to see.

As liberated as I had felt in the ChocolaTree, I found it difficult not to judge the couple on the rocks. I actually found them distracting. It was one thing to pick a nice spot for contemplation. It seemed rather arrogant to wade across the creek and prop yourself up on the rocks facing everyone else to take full lotus. There's meditating. Then there's *look at me meditating.*

In fact, it didn't take long before I was done listening to everyone around me openly discuss their take on the universe, aliens, chakras, and how open their third eye was after that session with so-and-so. It became more than distracting. It was down-right annoying. If one more person mentioned chakras, I was going to lose it. Seeking was draining. Something about it felt part soul-searching and part ego-gratifying. What part was I satisfying?

YOU CONSUME SO MUCH
  in the search for who you are
  You'll not find you there

21

NOT ALL MEDICINE WORKS FOR ALL PEOPLE

T ea and a muffin for the road. Anna and I headed into a local coffee shop before our drive to Cottonwood, west of Sedona. This was not the ChocolaTree. This was a local's coffee shop: mismatched chairs, dated wallpaper, old wooden counter. Still, a wall was covered with flyers and advertisements for spiritual counseling, chakra readings and tarot cards.

We paid for our traveling treats and then each drew a card from a dish near the cash register. *Of course* there were spiritual guidance cards at the counter. It was Sedona. I don't recall the message on my card. Not because it wasn't profound or pertinent to my search, but because it was something that made sense and morphed into all the other messages of my journey.

"What's your message?" I asked Anna.

"Tonglen," she replied.

"*Tong*len," I exaggerated.

Anna laughed. "Tonnnnnnnnnglen," she pitched her voice.

Then together we sang, "T-o-o-o-nglen." It was a great

word though we had no idea what it meant. We headed down the highway.

Just outside Cottonwood we found our meeting place. We shook hands with our guide and climbed into his truck. Well-tanned, as seemed the norm for the residents of the area, Cliff's long white-grey hair was neatly pulled into two braids, resting on the fronts of his shoulders. He wore a sleeveless red shirt and khaki pants with a small black leather pouch around his waist. His arms were lean and toned and his skin boasted a healthy glow.

"We'll head to the medicine wheel first," he said, "then on to the Shaman's Cave."

It was a short drive followed by an even shorter walk into the medicine wheel's location. Perched atop a ledge overlooking a deep valley to a wide, shrub-dotted plain on the other side and a low mountain range in the distance, the medicine wheel was a popular site with Spirit-seeking tourists.

I took up position on one of the stones forming the circle of the wheel. I placed the rental car keys and my phone at my feet. Anna sat across from me, with Cliff opposite her. We formed a triangle within the circle. The cloudless sky bolstered the desert heat. I wanted to crawl under the rock and seek shade like a rattlesnake, not sit on it and bake in the sun.

We closed our eyes to meditate and I dropped my head slightly. I felt Cliff and Anna's presence and their intensity of meditation, as if they were firmly fixed to the wheel. My head started to spin. I felt unwell and wanted to get out of the circle.

I held position and tried to settle within the wheel. I shifted from butt cheek to butt cheek, unable to steady my breath or my head. I wanted out of the wheel. It felt unhealthy to stay. I feared I would disturb the others if I got up and left but it was what I wanted more than anything. I forced myself to sit.

My phone rang. It hadn't rung since I left home, two days earlier, and rarely did I receive more than one call per week. I was mortified that I interrupted the sacred meditation with, of all things, my cell phone. I snatched it from the ground, noticing the number but not recognizing it, and switched the button to mute.

I returned it to my feet and resumed my forced position. My head pounded and every cell of my body screamed *please move!* My phone buzzed in the red dirt. You're kidding me. I grabbed the phone, mumbling how it must be an emergency and, excusing myself, walked away from the wheel and answered the call. It was Steve.

"Did you just call me?" I asked as I quickly put distance between me and the ear-shot of the others.

"Nope," he replied. "Just now. This is my first call."

I moved out of view so as not to disturb Anna and Cliff with my chat. I walked back toward the truck when an interesting tree caught my attention. It beckoned me and I approached it to find a natural archway in its branches. I stepped through and emerged in a scenic clearing with two large rocks in the center. I took a seat on one of them and finished my call, catching up on what Steve and the kids had been up to.

It had been difficult to leave my family to go Sedona. Many issues, not unfamiliar, had surfaced prior to leaving: the expense of the trip, leaving the kids, and Steve taking time off work, among them. But the year I had spent in yoga taught me that self-care wasn't selfish. When I took the time to fill my bucket, I could more easily (and happily) fill those of my family members.

I enjoyed hearing what Michael and Khali had been up to. When kids are young, if you blink, you miss milestones. And it was nice to hear Steve's voice, especially as a reprieve from the medicine wheel.

We said our goodbyes and I set my phone on the rock. It was quiet. It felt good to be away from the medicine wheel and the others. A sense of relief eased the remaining tension from my body. I pulled out my journal to jot down some musings from my tree-fenced porch. I sat, my back to the sun, overlooking the desert.

I laughed while I wrote how I hadn't had the courage to step out of the medicine wheel on my own, so a couple co-conspirators assisted me. I didn't know who belonged to that first call until I returned home to receive another call from her: my friend and spiritual co-seeker: the one who I left hanging in meditation at Fernando's. It seemed she and Steve had come to my rescue, tag-team style.

It felt spacious and easy on my solitary perch over-looking the Arizona landscape. My head felt as clear as the sky and the view. I could lay down and take a nice nap on the obliging rock. The medicine wheel may have been a sacred site, but it was not *my* sacred site. Alone on the rock, I slipped into bliss.

Voices emerged from the other side of the trees: the end to my hooky-playing. It's funny, hooky. It was something we did as kids to avoid the things we were *supposed* to do. What freedom came from those times! During my year in yoga, I had sought spirituality as a reprieve from the supposed to do of motherhood and family life. Now, in the middle of one of North America's most sacred sites, I welcomed family to save me from the supposed to do of spiritual seeking.

I made my way back from my secret clearing through the wild arbor. I thanked the local tree fellow who had shown me the way to the safe space. I saw Anna and Cliff walking from the wheel to the truck.

"I enjoyed a nice meditation on some rocks," I said, attempting to smooth any rough edges around the phone interruption. The air seemed a little tense but I opted to just fly by the awkwardness. "I didn't want to disturb you two again."

Cliff asked what we wanted to do with the remainder of our time. He gave us two options: Shaman's Cave and something obviously less appealing as I didn't care enough to hear it. Anna and I had come for the Shaman's Cave experience. We both felt pulled towards it. Cliff suddenly backtracked, realizing the time.

"It's a long drive to the Cave," he said. "It may be too much for today." Anna and I both spoke up, encouraging him to take us there. I could tell he had hoped for something closer, but Cliff agreed. We hopped back into his truck and continued our journey.

IF YOU WON'T LISTEN
   I will speak louder for you
   It's your choice to hear

22

GRASPING AT FEATHERS

We emerged from the red rock path, stepping foot on the Shaman's Dome and the top of the great rock. I caught my breath. I wasn't winded from the climb but in awe of the view. The backside of the rock, the path we hiked up, was misleading in its gradual, winding way. Standing on top of the dome I saw the height to which we had climbed, the drop below into the valley and the view of the red rock ranges in the distance.

The dome was smooth and large enough for the three of us to spread out in private reflection. A dent in the rock lent itself to a little pond of rainwater. I approached the mini oasis to find tiny feathers scattered about the rock near the water. I held them up for Cliff to see.

"Dove," he said.

Excited at my discovery, I gathered the most perfect of the feathers. Anna sat near the rock's edge meditating and Cliff stood opposite, overlooking the valley. I collected the white and grey feathers tossed about by the warm desert breeze. *I should sit and meditate.* The temptation of the feathers was too strong and I delighted in the dove's message as I gathered the sacred symbols.

I sat on the rock, soaking up the sun with the feathers tucked in my hand. I didn't feel like meditating, at least not what I had grown accustomed to as meditation – eyes fixed shut, seeking inward, waiting for a message, attempting to separate out the message from the mind chatter. I simply sat and enjoyed the pale blue sky resting on the ridges of red rocks, and the valley below rough with the shrubby whiskers of its five o'clock shadow.

"We should continue," Cliff nudged us from the warm silence of the dome rock. Anna and I stood and walked toward Cliff at the treed edge of the rock. We followed him along a shale path through wiry bushes. He stopped abruptly and turned to us.

"Look directly at the heels of the person in front of you," he said. "Don't lean into the rock. Stand straight up and place one foot in front of the other. Keep moving. Don't stop."

I half paid attention to him, fixing the feathers in my hand, ensuring I hadn't lost any along the way, when I noticed Anna was already far ahead of me. I couldn't follow her heels and stepped from the rocky path to the smooth, slanted red rock to catch up to her. A few steps out onto the rock and I understood Cliff's instructions were more of a warning.

My breath stuck in my chest. There was no room to take another gasp or step as I realized we had walked out onto the side of the great smooth rock, high above the valley floor. I collapsed into the rock, looking for something to grab onto. Fear had a firm grasp on my throat and tears began to well in my eyes. I felt the sting of rock scrape my knuckles, my hand refusing to let go of the feathers in exchange for my safety. This was not the ledge of Cathedral Rock the day before, where a fall may mean death or possibly only injury. This fall had no possible positive outcome.

I watched in disappointment as some of the feathers escaped my grasp, my knuckles bleeding. I clung to the sacred symbols tighter than I clung to the red rock. Would I exchange my life to hold on to a handful of symbolism?

Paralyzed by fear, my body pressed into the rock, one hand holding the smooth surface, the other gripping the feathers, my nails digging into the heal of my hand. Anna and Cliff out of sight, I knew I needed to move. I loosened fear's grip on my throat just enough to sip some air, the tears wetting my cheeks. I remembered all of Cliff's words. The heel cue could not help me. I thought about his warning to stand up straight, not lean into the rock.

I tried to lift myself. My legs shook uncontrollably, my stomach lurched. I stared at the feathers in my hand and suddenly knew that all would be okay. Even in my panic, I held on to the feathers, I held on to what I felt important, sacred, something greater that I didn't understand yet firmly grasped. The feathers should have all blown away as I instinctively grabbed for the wall to save myself, but they didn't. Because I didn't let go. I held faith in my hand and hope in my palm.

The paralysis subsided as an overwhelming sense of trust settled in. *The rock will take care of me. Spirit will take care of me.* I placed one foot in front of the other but could not manage to straighten myself from the rock wall. I walked along its steeply sloping side, as if I walked on air, suspended above the valley. I leaned hard onto the rock as I took step after step for what felt like hours.

I rounded a gentle corner and saw the cavernous opening, a small tree guarding it, and Anna, Cliff and Cliff's dog all inside, oblivious to my struggle. I heard my breath shakily escape the holding cell of my lungs as my foot found flatter terrain. I was not yet relieved as I didn't fully trust my trembling body to carry me smoothly to the opening.

I stepped up over the short retainer wall protecting the entrance of the cave and quickly wiped the tears from my face. I looked out over the valley as if I was enjoying the view, but I was remembering to breathe and thanking everything I could think of for giving me the strength to reach safety while overcome with my fear of heights. I did not want Cliff and Anna to know what had happened, to mar our experience with drama.

As I stood in gratitude at the mouth of the cave, something large and dark flew silently across the valley directly toward me. One large, black raven hung on the hot desert breeze. I stopped shaking, mesmerized in a moment with the raven, sharing the height of its flight from my place at the mouth of the cave.

I stepped back over the retaining wall, edging myself toward the small tree who guarded the ancient and sacred site in solitude. I plucked a strand of my hair and placed it at its roots in honour of its lone work. I thanked it for allowing me to come.

Cliff showed Anna the cave wall carving of a snake, but I didn't see it, still reeling from my walk. I half looked at the wall but couldn't make anything out. I opened my hand to count the remaining feathers, wet with the sweat of my palm. Four feathers remained: one for each direction. Anna placed a crystal in the side window of the cave; a perfect oval opening revealed the south valley view. I crossed the cave, placing a feather in each of the four directions, then took up a seat on the floor near the entrance and the shadow of an old fire. Remnants of sage and smudge remained.

I was not at ease, despite the pull of the cave's energy, the deep hum, the cool cave air, and the feeling of being safe in a red rock womb. I was not at ease because my mind reminded me that eventually I needed to leave the cave and would have to go back out onto the rock's slope. I tried to push the thought to the back of my mind and be present with the hallowed and spiritually-significant place where I sat.

The sound of a Native flute came from behind me and I turned to see Cliff peacefully playing in the throat of the cave. Anna sat near the window. I rode the music until it drove the adrenaline from my body. I closed my eyes and inhaled the notes on the cool cave air. I felt Anna. I felt her in meditation. The deliberate meditation. Everything intensified in the cave. The flute's trance-inducing melody washed strongly over me. The cave's cold permeated my skin. Anna's silent seeking encroached on me like a breaking wave.

I couldn't find my meditation. Either the exhaustion which followed the panic and fear and adrenaline of my walk, or the cave — one of them, perhaps both — wouldn't let me. I sat with the taste of tears in my mouth and the cold cave floor on my boney bum. Suddenly a man stood in front of me. He looked Aztec or perhaps Mayan, I couldn't tell, but he reminded me of someone I studied in high school.

He stood before me, yet at eye level. His hair was pure black, shiny and the same length from above his eyes, atop his ears and around the back of his head. His eyes captivated me as I watched them morph, as he morphed, into an owl, wings stretched to the side, atop a totem pole. He became the totem pole.

I tried to communicate with him. *Who are you? What do you want me to know?* I felt I could not understand and yet, to receive such a powerful vision in a sacred place, there had to be a way I could know what he came to tell me. His eyes were carved deep into the wood and lured me as though they were the secret, the message. They weren't really his eyes though, more his brow arches, like archways to another place. Archways that could transport me to another dimension, through the eyes that were there yet not.

A gust of wind rushed through the south window, sending Anna's crystal loudly pinging to the cave floor, pulling Cliff abruptly from his flute and Anna and me from our trances, like a gong sounded by a master. A raven rose on the wind at the mouth of the cave and cawed at us. We looked at one another. Chills stroked my skin, pushing goosebumps to the surface. Anna's eyes were as wide as I felt my own to be and she reached for her long, fragile, clear crystal, surprisingly still intact after its fall.

I started filing every detail of my vision to memory, replaying it over and over so as not to miss anything. Cliff packed up his flute while Anna and I took a moment to say our goodbyes to the cave. I stepped over the short retainer wall at the entrance, placing my hand on the lone guardian tree in gratitude for its service. Cliff, Anna and I all left the cave and walked out onto the sloping red wall.

Within, what felt like a few steps, my feet were back on the shrubby path. I stopped, turning back toward the mouth of the cave which I could no longer see from my place on the path, concealed once again. I looked down at the sloping red rock that had previously paralyzed me in fear. It didn't seem the same path. It was an effortless path, an easy path, devoid of fear. Quick and steady.

We made our way back to Cliff's truck, passing a sweaty,

overheated hiker seeking the cave. Cliff stopped to give directions and talk to the hiker who had been told to park way down the trail, hours I would have guessed — once we passed his vehicle on the return — from the site of the cave. *Poor guy.* Seemed the cave made him work harder for his journey. Though one could say I worked equally hard for mine. The cave required initiation prior to entry. A facing-of-fears. A purification. A commitment perhaps.

We headed back along the gravel roads to Cliff's house and our rental car, me in the passenger seat and Anna in the backseat with Cliff's dog. Cliff inserted a CD into the dusty dash and sang along with the song he had written and recorded. I leaned back, sinking into my seat for the long drive. The warm wind from the open window pushed my hair away from my face. The red rock dust swirled behind the truck as we traversed the landscape. I sank into Cliff's song and the desert's arms, the kiss of the Shaman's Cave lingered on my lips.

YOU CRAVE a message
  You must first unlock the door
  The key is inside

23

NATURE'S CHURCH

I t was impressive, to say the least. As our rental car crested the hill, we began to appreciate the scale of the work in front of us. The Chapel of the Holy Cross was breath-taking. I had no desire initially to visit the site. I was more interested in nature's church than man's. I had a long-running struggle with religion.

Most people who know me don't know that I prayed every night as a girl. I always knew we were part of something bigger. I went to church until age five and then only at Christmas or Easter with my Grandmother after that. I liked the singing and the sense of community. I liked the gathering after the sermon. I can still smell the welcoming blend of coffee, baked goods, sandwiches, and mustiness of the Presbyterian church's basement kitchen. I see the ladies put out the teacups, happily visiting with one another like family.

I didn't always like the sermon, though that depended on the Reverend delivering it. Church had a way of feeling both communal and constricting. I never wanted to believe in someone else's beliefs. I wanted to know myself through my experience. I wanted to know life and the universe through my senses. I wanted to wrestle and reason and invite perspectives and possibilities of my own.

And I had no care for a system that would pit one religion against another. It is one Earth. How could we be so divided and live in the same house? But I still felt a greater presence, a greater force and many forces within that force. We believed for a long time that the world was flat. It always made me wonder what else we believe in error.

Conversations about religion or God always made me cringe. They made me want to go sit outside and commune with nature. They made me uncomfortable because I didn't know. I didn't have any answers on the subject. I didn't know Jesus. I had no direct experience with any of the main characters in the bible. It was hard to weigh in on something I'd never touched.

But nature, I could weigh in on that. I could weigh in on the smell of the earth in a spring rain, the warmth of a chinook breeze across my face, or the leaves whispering the wind's words. Even in my visions I knew nature. I knew the Native women washing their hair in the stream. I knew the deer nibbling wild grasses in the birch trees. I knew the feeling of shivers up my spine and joy in my heart as the air around me fills with a density of energy I can only name as Spirit.

But the arguing over God and Jesus and how to live your life according to scripture: I knew nothing of that. I had many questions as a girl and had read the Bible cover-to-cover at the age of thirteen – the age when, in many traditions, I would have gone on a vision quest to find the answers to my questions. I had enjoyed several of the Bible's passages but found no answers to my questions there.

Who are we? Where did we come from? What are we doing

here? Where are we supposed to go? What is the point of all of this? Where does our consciousness come from and what happens after we die? This can't be all we are here to do. You know, the usual questions of a thirteen-year-old.

I tended to avoid churches unless they were historical. I loved wandering through the Cathedrals of Europe and listening to their stories. Who had walked where I walk, what people came? I loved the stain-glass windows and the grand ceilings. Great stories. Old stories.

Anna and I walked up the long winding ramp to the Holy Cross. My new friend, Cathedral rock, stood in the distance. I surveyed the looming red rock wall behind the Chapel. It was said to host a rocky outcropping that looked exactly like an eagle. I studied the grooves and patterns, searching for this winged rock Guardian. I spotted him, curved beak and sharp eyes, overlooking the sacred site.

I snapped pictures of the gardens near the top of the walkway, with their stone angel sculptures and humming-bird feeders. I thought of my grandmother. I sat on a stone bench. I could feel her sitting on the bench with me enjoying the view. Funny – it was Nan, who passed years earlier, with whom I enjoyed going to church. And here I sat with her again.

Anna was reading something on the outside wall of the Chapel. I headed toward her, stopping to admire an ornate art stone embedded in the ground at the entrance. Tiny tiles of blue, white and red gave shape to a white dove with an olive branch, laid at my feet. The mosaic greeted me. I snapped a picture and then moved on to the sign on the wall that Anna had been reading.

The sign told the story of the Chapel, which looked like a cave above ground. A wall of windows filled the square entrance sided by concrete slabs. The garden was quaint and serene. The view was spectacular. It was, however, the story on that plaque on the outside wall of the entrance that hooked me. The plaque's title read "HOW THE CHAPEL CAME INTO BEING *by Marguerite Brunswig Staude*"

It was Marguerite's story. Suddenly there was a person behind the sacred art: a woman. She walked the red rocks. She envisioned the Chapel. For many years she envisioned the Chapel and Sedona was not her first choice. She had tried repeatedly to bring her vision to life. It finally found a home amongst the red rocks.

When Marguerite gave the chapel to the Catholic Church, she instructed that there be no services held there. "She wanted the Chapel to be a place to pray, reflect and find God through the beauty of art." * Marguerite Brunswig Staude in *Arizona Women's Heritage Trail.* I thought about her story. It brought the chapel to life for me. I couldn't wait to step inside.

Anna had already moved into the structure. I took only a few steps inside and then stopped, in awe at the standing piece of art I occupied. The window at the front of the Chapel was like a window on the desert. It framed the red rocks and blue sky as the one delivering the sermon at the front of the Chapel.

"Look here," it offered. "Look out over this vast, open place, this sacred land, this art of nature. See the divine here."

I walked past the rows of lit candles in red candle holders and people raising match to candle for loved ones. I sat on the front pew. I pried my eyes from the view in order to take in the interior of the Chapel. Anna sat on the row across the aisle, head bowed. I closed my eyes for a moment's meditation.

Jesus stood before me. Just like that, in a flash I was

pulled into another reality; a clear and lucid vision. My chest hurt. Something squeezed my heart. Or maybe my heart pushed back against the walls around it. Tears flooded my eyes and an immense wave of love overtook me. It was a sample, all I could bear to receive; a small taste of the purest, most forgiving force. I knew if I stayed much longer or felt the full force, it would consume me, and my heart would burst from its inability to perceive or receive all that it felt.

Mother Mary quickly stepped to his side as if to both comfort me and assure me that it was indeed Jesus. Along with my fractured relationship with the church came my equally constrained idea of Jesus. Same deal: I'd never met Him, so I had a hard time developing a relationship with the idea of Him.

The love that I felt, that I'd tasted, was beyond measure. It almost seemed beyond what could be possible in human form, yet desperately needed, and perhaps what was originally intended. I understood how the power of love was at once frightening and desired. That level of vulnerability, of forgiveness, of complete compassion caused physical pain in my body, yet was the most humbling and beautiful moment. Like the birth of a child.

I reached up to wipe the tears from my eyes and realized they were never closed. Jesus and Mary stood at the front of the Chapel. And then they were gone. Tourists chatted excitedly at the entrance behind me, unaware of the sparse few meditators in the pews. I took a couple deep, cleansing breaths and allowed my eyes to connect with Anna's. My heart still hurt as I made my way back to Nan and the stone seat near the garden.

I spent years trying to reconcile my relationship with religion. I had many rational and emotional standpoints on that debate. What I would come to realize, years after my visit to the Chapel – in fact right after writing this chapter – was that I wasn't angry about religion. It was as if God was taken from me. I went to Sunday School as a kid —though I remember hating it. I wanted to sit out front with the adults. When my parents divorced, we no longer went to church. I don't believe Nan had to cajole me to join her. I wanted to.

I liked the thought of God. I liked the feeling of not being alone, of a greater force in the universe. It felt right to me as a child. When I read the Bible cover-to-cover at age thirteen, I wasn't looking for answers. I was looking for God. I was looking for that connection that was severed when I no longer attended church. I prayed in secret and silence every night until my late twenties. God didn't grow up in my home and I felt I could not talk about it.

The experience at the Chapel of the Red Rock gave me the opportunity to meet God on my terms later in life. To reconcile a relationship with Spirit. To seek connection within and without, to something greater, to some source of it all. But I needed to understand my strained relationship with religion and God and Jesus. I needed to admit that the separation I felt at a young age caused pain and resulted in my desire to seek out Source, though it showed up as confusion and resentment for most of my life.

I NEVER LEFT you
   I have so much love for you
   You must love yourself

24

STAR STRUCK

"I'm not sure we'll make it," said Anna.

"Oh, we'll make it, alright," I replied, pressing the pedal closer to the floor. I always rent SUVs. Especially when I'm near the mountains. Heading up the bumpy, flood-cracked, gravel road to Schnebly, I confirmed my choice of SUV even in the temperate climate of Arizona. The vehicle snaked around each corner of the switchback. The sun was setting fast and Anna and I aimed for a sunset on the red rocks to cap our Sedona adventure.

Where to park? Where to park? Fuck it. I pulled off the road and threw the SUV into park, half in the ditch. "Run for it!" We darted through the scrub brush and onto the vast, smooth rocks. We raced across the expanse of open terrain high on the hillside like a couple of track athletes, bounding up ledges and racing over the rocks, chasing the sun.

We snapped a couple quick photos together before Anna headed for the edge. I wandered around the middle, marveling at the light of the sun igniting the rocks. Orange glowed all around us. I stood, face to the sun's setting rays and the strong west winds. I leaned in as the wind pushed my hair off my face. If I'd had wings, I would have opened them and hung, motionless in the air.

My shadow stood large behind me and I pulled out my phone to capture the magic. We had made it in time. Sunset on the red rocks and our final evening. What a ride.

I sat on the rocks, now taking on deep rusts and reds in the quickening of the fading light. I couldn't close my eyes. Who would want to? The desert stretched out at my feet, the sun spread across the blue sky before me.

There was magic in that sunset. Rainbow in its rays. Colours pulsed outward from its center and lit the landscape. Low on the horizon, I could gaze directly at the sun. Red and green danced around it. Blue and yellow. The sun had its own aura, its chakra body, and I saw more than just the light of its rays.

My cheeks ached from the smile on my face. My whole body was lit from nature. I was high on the wild wind, the crimson rocks, the endless darkening sky and the height of the red rock playground.

The sun drops fast in the desert. And when it's gone, darkness moves swiftly, unlike the Rocky Mountain sunsets where dusk hangs in the air for hours before darkness slowly chases it across the sky to the west in their endless game of tag.

Anna walked toward me with a smile that equaled mine. "What the fuck, Steph? Could it get any better than this?" We hugged on our field of rock.

"We'd better move it," I released my grip on her lean frame. "It'll be hard to find our way back soon." We flew across the rocks, shoulder-checking the last of the sunset while we searched for the vehicle before the darkness engulfed our path.

Giddy from yet another mind-blowing communion with

the magic that is Sedona, we paused to draw hearts in the red dust that covered the ground between bushes. I took a final dusky photo of a pristine agave and then we left Schnebly.

Schnebly wasn't done with us yet. As we wound back down the bumpy road toward the town, a giant shooting star magnetized our gaze.

"Holy shit!" I slammed on the brakes. The ball of light was in the earth's atmosphere. It burned brighter and brighter with a long tail behind it.

"I don't think that's a shooting star," said Anna. We sat, glued to it, as if we watched a comet pass our seat on the highest peak on the planet.

The celestial visitor shot across the vast black canvas before us. The hairs on the back of my neck stood at attention. It was immense and we were immensely excited and inspired by the visitor.

"Let's head back to our cabin and grab blankets," offered Anna. "We can park up our hill and watch the sky."

"Yes! I saw the perfect spot to park when I first arrived."

At the cabin, we gathered blankets and pulled on sweaters.

"I put the kettle on for tea," I grabbed my travel mug and Anna handed me hers.

We drove up the road from our rental accommodation to find the perfect place to park, away from street lights or town lights. We laid one blanket across the hood of the vehicle, which felt toasty warm on our bums from the engine heat. We grabbed our teas and sat on the hood, covering ourselves with the other blanket.

Anna and I reclined against the windshield, gazing at the stars.

"Stephy, I've never told anyone this..." Anna confided in me.

"Oh, An, thank you for telling me. I must tell you..." And I entrusted her with my secrets. We deepened our friendship, deepened our connection to one another, as we deepened our connection to nature, Spirit, and the magic of Sedona. We never saw another star as impressive as the Shnebly sighting, but we remained for a long time in our open-air observatory.

THANK you for coming
I send you off with fireworks
You who trusted me

25

WHEN YOU THINK NO ONE'S LOOKING

I dug my toes into the cold sand and dropped into Warrior II. My right hand stretched toward the ocean and the darkened horizon. My left hand pointed to the handful of early-rising, gawking resort tourists. I found myself, as usual, trying to find a balance between the sacred and society. I resisted reaching forward, leaning into the waves and the whisper of the breeze off the water. I remained mindful of my center, reluctantly drawing myself back toward the resort.

There weren't many people about in the early morning hours but enough to steer my practice. When I knew no one was looking, my practice took on whatever form my heart and my surroundings dictated. I could let go and get lost in the moment, which usually ended with streaming tears of gratitude.

On the public resort beach, I presented myself as a simple tourist enjoying a bit of yoga in the sand. I inhaled the cool air off the ocean's surface, exhaling love and gratitude for the opportunity to commune with her in the first hours of light. My gaze fixed on the horizon, it was difficult not to be distracted by tourists in my periphery.

A jogger on a beach rarely warranted a second glance but somehow a girl in Warrior II drew direct stares. As I reached in opposite directions, I held the gift of the magical Hawaiian Islands in one hand, and in the other, an awkward discomfort of a yoga spectacle on the beach. I breathed into the place in between.

It was April. Nature school had led me to Maui: a gift I gratefully received. The whole family traveled this time. They were all asleep in the hotel room while I took up morning practice on the beach.

After five nights at the resort, and equal mornings playing sandy yoga statue on the beach, we moved on to the Olowalu house and the universe handed me a basket of gifts. The house sat on the most pristine piece of land overlooking the ocean and the two islands of Lanai and Molokai. No tourists for miles.

A twenty-five-foot mango tree teasingly dangled bright orange and red ripe fruit from its out-of-reach branches. Ripe mangoes lay torn open near its base: a sweet feast for the local birds. The house, with its extensive, green, wooden front porch that ran the entire ocean side of the building, was more luxurious inside than the pictures online had conveyed.

The stairs up the porch led to double glass entry doors which opened into a central living space with vaulted ceiling, several teak chairs and couch with coffee table. A huge kitchen with a granite-topped central island filled nearly a third of the home's living space. The kids each enjoyed a spacious bedroom with wooden window shutters for enhanced island character. I walked into the master suite. Its pineapple-carved four-post bed and bright white linens were a welcome invitation. Windows wrapped the entire ranch-style bungalow, providing a generous supply of natural light and ocean views. Palm trees dotted the expanse of lawn. I dropped my bags and darted for the shoreline.

There was no beach, no sand to speak of. Rocks, shells, coral, and driftwood met the water at the land. It was a beachcomber's paradise. The best gift in the basket was the old private pier: a concrete extension of the rocky shoreline, used by the old sugar plantation built in 1922 that neighboured the property on the other side of the trees.

More tempting than the mango tree, the pier called me out to its furthest point. A cement bench sat at its end and as I sat on the bench, facing back toward the shore and the house, I realized I was the furthest point out from the island. I could see the entire shoreline on the northwest side. With Lanai and Molokai standing knee-deep in the ocean behind me, the pier provided the widest perspective on the island. It was as if I sat with Grandmother Ocean herself, detached from the land.

Here, I could get lost in the moments again. On the pier no one would distract me from diving deeply into my surroundings. I decided to wake early each morning, not wasting an opportunity to sit with the ocean and the island before the sun woke them both. *What wisdom lives here?*

I WOKE THE NEXT MORNING, excited to take my place on the pier, only to discover another in that place. It seemed I wasn't the only one who felt the sacredness of the pier. A woman sat in meditation on the bench. My bench. Agitated by the perception of a lost opportunity, I had to honour the practice of the woman and I gave her space as I slowly made my way along the shoreline, opting to collect shells instead.

I hadn't thought about the tide and was pleasantly surprised by the wider morning shoreline and the many deposits the ocean had made in the night. Shells of every colour, design, and size lay at my feet. Coral comprised the shore, with new pieces locking into place on the tropical puzzle.

The odd coconut shell and flip flop beached themselves among the ocean floor debris, and pieces of smooth, coloured glass washed up like a gallery exhibit of the ocean's vast art collection. I was so engulfed in the exploration I didn't see the woman leave the bench until she approached me, bag in hand.

She reached into her bag and handed me three pristine pieces of coral. She had a trained eye, that of someone who spent many morning hours on the shoreline, and her pieces were coral perfection. She gave them to me. She told me she and her husband came to the pier regularly.

They lived on the other side of the island but came most mornings. He put in his boat and went fishing while she enjoyed the morning on the shore. Any agitation lingering from the theft of my morning meditation on the bench dissolved with her generosity and her friendliness. It was the perfect way to enjoy my first morning at Olowalu.

Subsequent mornings brought more beachcombing. It became my favourite meditation; eyes fixed softly on the rocky beach, allowing unique objects to pop into my view from the dense oceanic collage. Pieces of shellfish wedged under rocks. Most shells didn't resemble their former glory, worn away by the ocean's repeated strokes as she polished glass and rock. Small, black crabs scattered back and forth across the pier's end, playing tag with the spray.

The Olowalu house itself offered many gifts. Not only in its views, comforts, and kitchen size but the coffee table books proved extraordinary. The owners of the home obviously had a love of original Hawaiian works. Many of the books heralded tales of the islands and their inhabitants.

One book, in particular, leapt into my lap: a book of ancient Hawaiian healing chants and their uses. What were the odds that I would reserve a holiday home that held ancient healing lessons? I felt as if the island wished to teach me its secrets to add to the ever-growing body of sacred wisdom the earth shared with me. Gratitude and humility swelled inside as I read the words on the pages and spoke the blessings aloud, hoping my pronunciation did them justice.

The book revealed plant medicines used by Hawaiian healers. It described the plant, its use, and blessings to assist in healing. As I read various healing prayers, one prayer played on my tongue. I put it into practice immediately with my daughter, Khali, and her sudden fever. I wrote that particular chant in my journal. Humbled by the gift, I did not wish to take more than I needed off the island. I didn't wish to be greedy or disrespectful of the gift and the traditions. I recorded the name and author of the book, knowing that if it was to stay with me then I would find it and buy my own copy.

I wandered across the property, toward the greatest of the old palm trees. The lone giant stood watch between the ocean and the land. He was magnificent, with a trunk that could only be hugged by several people joining hands to wrap the width of its considerable base. I wanted to commune with the elder tree but as I approached, I felt a wall between the tree and me.

I felt the tree warn me not to approach. He said his

wisdom was for elders and I was not advanced enough in my practice or spiritual maturity to commune with him. Disappointed, I knew better than to disregard the message and I respected the old tree, giving him a wide birth as I stayed nearer the pier and the ocean.

I collected shells as yet another woman occupied my bench. I watched her, of course pretending not to, as she left the bench and walked straight to a slimmer palm on the center of the property. She hugged it before disappearing into a path in the trees.

I approached the younger palm, which stood a good twenty feet in the air. How had I not noticed this tree before? I was preoccupied with the elder, with the grandest of teachers, and the less ornate friend had slipped my attention. I placed my hands on the rough trunk and stilled my mind to hear.

What a happy young fellow, this tree. I touched my forehead to him and we connected in laughter and in tears. Another gift of the property and the ancients. He spoke about the old tree, the elder one that was not yet meant for me. He said it was not personal, that I would not understand the lessons of the old tree, and that the old tree would just not speak to me.

I felt okay with my younger companion, whose energy was more suited to mine. The elder tree felt serious and powerful, too much pressure for my tender energy, still raw from its birth into these strange realms. My young friend was light-hearted and communication with him felt easy. I enjoyed his company, as I enjoyed the company of all the island's plant and animal friends.

At the end of my year in yoga, almost exactly one year earlier, we were guided by our facilitator, Alora, to blindly choose one item from a bucket list we had written. When I had reached into the hat to pull a strip of paper, I pulled *dance the hula in Hawaii*. It wasn't until I stood on the stage of the luau later that day with Khali and Michael learning the hula, that I remembered the bucket list pull. It was nothing I had planned. The universe had conspired to fulfill my selected bucket choice.

Steve and I also danced that night, at the luau with the kids. We danced to celebrate our anniversary. The next day, we took the kids to the secret beach where we had been married nine years earlier. That day of our wedding was pure perfection.

The tide was high this time, much higher than when we'd wed. It nearly washed us all away. We continued our Aloha adventure with lavender tea and scones with mango jelly at the lavender farm, surrounded by stunning flora and statues of Buddha. We visited the I'ao Valley Needle: home of worship and place of burial to Hawaiian royals. If I was going to learn anything of my purpose, the ancient and sacred sites must be able to help. If I couldn't find myself where medicine men and women, and great rulers once honoured, then where?

ON THE FINAL evening at Olowalu House, Steve and I walked the pier while the kids ran around the lawn. A man had been sitting on the bench. He moved to lay on the rocks by the time we reached the end of the pier. His bike lay near him and he appeared as though he had been there for some time, enjoying the sacred spot. I didn't wish to disturb him but wanted one last sunset from my cherished perspective on the island. Steve and I said hello as we approached and he nodded to us with a smile: an older Asian fellow, perhaps in his sixties. I noticed his headphones and realized he lay listening to music. That must be enchanting music, I thought, to want to hear it more than the soul-soothing sounds of the waves, the birds and the island breeze in the fronds.

We left him to his special place and made our way back toward the house, photographing each other with the palm trees. Steve and the kids headed inside, and I sat on the front step watching the fellow on the pier, the boats in the distance, and the orange clouds brushing Lanai and Molokai.

Suddenly the fellow popped up and began to dance. He appeared to be dancing for the ocean, perhaps the islands in the distance as well. He put on quite the show and as I zoomed my camera in to catch him, I saw the enormous smile on his face while he performed. He shook his shoulders at the island and his butt at the ocean and then turned around for a Hollywood game show-style finale kiss that he threw out across the water.

I felt his love for the island, his joy, and gratitude expressed in his celebratory dance. I felt his courage and conviction in his practice of honouring that which gave him his smile. I didn't know his name nor his story, but I felt his life force. A beautiful soul, I smiled in gratitude for being a member of the audience for this heartfelt show. I knew he didn't do it for anyone else and he didn't care who saw. I knew he would do his dance even if resort tourists looked on, even if the whole world watched.

I took over seven hundred photos on our vacation, seventy percent of which were of plants, birds, animals, and sunsets. Only thirty percent were of the kids. Though I enjoyed my family and our holiday together, I felt compelled by the plants, the healing wisdom of the ancients and the island, and a growing wave about to carry me to a distant shore if I surfed it well.

Hawaii was one of our most memorable family holidays. And another in a string of gifts from the earth as I travelled from mountains to red rocks to ocean and island expanding my knowledge in the school of nature. I had covered a lot of ground in six months.

Obsessed by experiencing more of the realm of Spirit, energy, ancient wisdom, healing, and nature, coincidences seemed to abound, leaving me breadcrumbs along the trail to what I hoped was my life's one true purpose. I interpreted the presence of the books on ancient healing practices and chants, along with my encounters with the trees, as big crumbs. I just didn't know what to do with them.

I returned home and, after a brief reunion with my cat and emptying of suitcases into the washing machine, jumped onto my laptop to research the old book and place an order. The book was no longer in print with no copies to be found. I laughed out loud. *Of course it's not available.* I thanked the ancients once again for the perfect holiday with my family, for taking great care of us, and for the wisdom piece that was meant for me.

The one prayer I had written, practiced and adopted as my own, was the only one meant to come home. The one prayer, used by Hawaiian healers with plant medicine, that I in turn used on my daughter to ease her fever — and my worry — returned with me. I kept it sacred and practiced it often. In the spirit of Aloha.

It's not a business
   The spirit of Aloha
   is a way of life

PART III

PRACTICUM

26

THE PLANT GUIDE

I walked Two-toed Pond. I greeted my friends, the three trees, on the path. I leaned against the one standing on his own on the south side. As I closed my eyes, the ocean view from the front lawn of the Olowalu house flashed before me. It was my friend, the young palm tree. Somehow the trees communicated with one another; one was a bridge to the other: Mother Nature's great telephones.

I felt so happy to see my Hawaiian friend and asked him to say hello to the ocean for me. I poured forth my love and gratitude for him. *I miss you*. I could see it all as if I stood beside him. I thanked my pond tree friend for that gift and every time I returned to Two-toed, I paused to connect with both my local and island friends.

Life at home became magical. Helpful conversations with lovely people occurred most places I went. I began manifesting via online shopping, finding just what I wanted, when I wanted it and on sale. I would think about something and receive an email or flyer offering that very thing: courses, classes, books, clothing. Which began to pose a problem: what I thought about most was trying to find my purpose, and since I didn't have any clear idea of what that was, I looked for it everywhere, manifesting a myriad of opportunities usually left incomplete.

Shopping for groceries one day, a potted plant captured my attention. I set down my basket of gluten-free finds, face-to-leaf with a small green being. The label read: lemon balm. I plucked it from its display perch and took it home, placing it on the window sill in the kitchen.

When I smelled the plant, it gave off no noticeable aroma. When I rubbed the leaves, however, the tiny hairs on the leaf-fronts released the most delightful lemon scent. It lingered on my fingers, uplifting, fresh and warm.

A quick tour of the internet provided ample research on my new friend. Initially a favourite of Greece, by the 15th century lemon balm was used by most of Europe as a general tonic and for many ailments, and, consistent with the times, particularly popular when infused in wine. She was widely used for longevity when consumed regularly. I enjoyed one single leaf each morning in warm water for tea. I had begun a love affair with lemon balm.

I liked to call her by her proper name, Melissa, for Melissa Officinalis, and Greek for *bee*. Her leaves were soft and covered in fine hairs that contained most of her essential oils. I twisted them gently as I placed one in my mug, covering it with warm water. I happily inhaled the lemony steam from my cup. Her fresh earthy-lemon taste soothed me as I enjoyed sip after sip, standing in my kitchen each morning.

I pulled out a piece of paper and wrote *Mélisse* on the page, French for Melissa. I added *Soothe your senses with lemon balm and lavender.* I wrote it in green and drew a lavender sprig for the l in Mélisse. I looked at my artwork, unsure from where it had sprung.

I envisioned tisanes, herbal teas, with lemon balm and lavender. An herbal wave washed over me. It was all I could think about. I researched organic suppliers for the best herbs. The more I thought about Mélisse, the more plants appeared that wanted to join in the fun.

Rose came. Then orange blossom. Violet joined in and I found myself no longer listening to the kids talk to me from the backseat of the car on the drive to school, instead blends and synergies of plants danced in my head. *Ylang ylang and lavender!* I thought about infusing the plants in oils and creating the purest, most sensual body care. I spent three hours pouring over the list of wholesale herbs and placed my first order — which had grown from my initial muse to include a variety of dried organic herbs, luxurious carrier oils, and premium essential oils.

I couldn't stop myself and I didn't want to. I had no idea what to do with all the energy and ideas flowing through me; my obsession with the plants. I had been back from Hawaii only a week and felt possessed by some strange creative energy.

I received an email, days after my shipment, from a clinic I had never heard of. It was their newsletter and I scrolled through to see if I knew anyone at the clinic, looking for a connection as to why I received the email. The newsletter advertised an upcoming four-week session entitled *Herbal Medicine Primer*, including an herb walk in the mountains on the final session.

I forwarded the email to Anna, adding "seriously??!!" in the subject line. It seemed the bread crumb trail continued. I signed up for the course which started two weeks later. Apparently, the universe knew I liked the fast-track, no time to hesitate or change my mind.

I learned hands-on methods for infusing herbs in oils,

making tinctures with alcohol, and the most intimidating for me: beeswax balms. Of course, by this time I knew my fortune in attracting great teachers and the Naturopathic Doctor that guided our studies was funny, brilliant, awake, and equally surprised by how I came to receive her email since their office policy was to send only to existing clients.

After the third session of the course I received a package on my doorstep. I opened it like a five-year-old on Christmas morning. I sat on the hardwood floor in the entryway reefing on the packing tape until it gave way. I didn't even bother to fetch a knife or move the package away from the front door.

I inhaled the inside of the box, then smelled each bag one by one, followed by each oil. I couldn't remember feeling so happy and yet still did not know what I was to do with all I had just purchased. I jotted ideas down in a journal.

The night before our final session and mountain herb-walk, I received a gift dream. A yellow plant came to me. It showed me how it was filled with liquid gold light, then it showed me how I was filled with this same gold. I had never seen the plant before and didn't know its name.

It told me "goldenrod" and I wrote it down when I woke, intending to research it to see if it did indeed exist. I rushed out of the house that morning, after getting breakfast together for the kids, and forgot about the research. I headed to the meetup of my herbal group in the mountains.

We hiked the main trail, stopping regularly to identify, discuss, and often taste the local flora. There were a few plants I recognized from my walks with the coulee — though this time, no stories revealed themselves. I didn't expect to see visions on our herb walk. I assumed the stories were between me and the coulee.

On our way in I spotted a plant up high on the cliff. I thought it was fascinating how it grew from the rocks on the mountainside – resourceful and resilient — but I didn't ask its name. I continued on with the group.

I discovered that wild juniper berries are delicious, if the bears have left any. I jotted notes in my phone to research later: bears and juniper berries. There were too many plants to remember. Fortunately, only a few were toxic, however toxic enough that you'd have only once chance to not remember which they were.

On our way out, someone else noticed the plant on the cliff, "What's that plant called?"

"Goldenrod," replied our guide. I stopped short. I scaled the narrow ledge where the plant perched, without thinking about the height, the logistics of getting to it or back down for that matter, or the fact that I was in a provincial park and needed to stay on the trail. I'd already shit in one park, what was a little off-trail excursion in another? Within seconds, moved by sheer will and excitement, I perched next to the golden plant of my dreams.

When I had taken my raw nutrition certification, my teacher said that our evolution is tied to the plants and their evolution tied to us. I was beginning to realize that plants are talking. All the time they're talking. We just never sit still long enough to listen. They have stories to tell and they want to connect with us. Considering the state of the planet, it seems to me it's not so much our *evolution* that is bound together, but our survival.

WE ARE BOUND to you
  Everything you need is here
  Please listen to us

27

HERBAL INTERNSHIP

I worked with each plant individually. Though I got to know them one by one, Melissa held a special place in my heart as my first teacher. I continued to surf my laptop for any intriguing details about the green dame.

She was said to help soothe the nerves and lift the spirits. In times of grief, Melissa was a master comforter. Also soothing for an upset or nervous stomach, she held calming properties, easing worry and anxiety and encouraging restful sleep. My continued research touted her use to reduce fevers in children brought on by cold and flu, and the addition of fresh leaves to salads and sauces for flavour and aroma.

I found a sixteenth-century way of working with herbal remedies: a tea would be brewed, and the pot poured into the bath to soak in while a cup of the tea was consumed during the bath. The method intrigued me, and I put it into practice immediately with Melissa.

I poured the delicate yellow tea into my bath and my mug, sank into the warm water and sipped away. Deep therapy ensued. My entire body, mind and soul softened in the lemony liquid. While I released into Melissa's nurturing embrace, herbal inspiration continued to bubble up around me. I envisioned a line of herbal teas called *Sip and Soak Tisanes*.

Rosa came next. She belonged to a large extended family. Her reputation was legendary, and according to google, history captured this beautiful blossom over and over again. I always had a sweet spot for rose as the Alberta roses grew wild through the bushes of my childhood home. They also grow along the hillside of my adult home, above the coulee and along Two-toed Pond. Few scents compare to the sweet Alberta rose. Her fragrance says "You can't tame me. You can't cultivate me. You must be here when I come. Catch me in the moment. Inhale deeply then let me go."

Pure love: the rose's energy. Shades of pink for self-love and care. Deep reds of lovers and love expressed. The pure white of innocence. Yellow of friendship, joy and forgiveness. A flower of heart chakra, the rose nurtures gently, deeply, and completely.

I opened the bag of rose petals from my shipment and the unmistakable scent spilled out along with delicate red petals. I closed my eyes and breathed deeply, drawing rose energy into my cells. Sensual. Warm. Earthy. Womanly. Soft. Powerful. My body opened to the feeling of rose.

I investigated her origins. [1]My research revealed rose was thirty-five million years old, with over one hundred and fifty species. *Thirty-five million years old! That's a long lineage of love; an enduring presence on the planet.* Fossils were found in the United States, but some guessed her age as even older than stated. The oldest rose known today is Rosa Gallica or French rose. The Damask rose is a descendant of this original rose.

From hieroglyphics to the tombs of Egypt, Renaissance

prose to wedding ceremonies, Rosa has held a prominent place in history. In the seventeenth century rose and rose water were considered legal tender in Europe.

One of the best known and most expensive of the essential oils, rose was one of the first plants to be successfully distilled almost 1000 years ago. [2]It may take up to 242,000 rose petals to distill 5ml of pure rose oil, hence the value and a compelling reason to enjoy rose petal-infused oils, instead of essential oil, as a more sustainable and economic indulgence.

The Greeks, Romans and Arabs used the precious oils for centuries in perfumes, cosmetics and medicines. I discovered that the properties of the rose oil are as extensive as her history. Used as an aphrodisiac, antidepressant, antiviral, to calm inflammation, balance hormones, fade scars and stretch marks, soothe menstrual cramps, tone and lift the skin; rose was a popular choice. She seemed to lend herself to all things feminine.

The petals were reported to make a nourishing infusion or tea to drink, providing gentle purification and detox of the stomach, liver and uterus. Infused in a carrier oil, the petals of rose were claimed to soften skin. Suitable for all skin types, rose was most known for nurturing sensitive, dry or mature skin.

Rosehip seed oil was credited with reducing wrinkles and signs of premature aging, improving scars, reducing redness and hydrating skin. I researched modern-day use but was more intrigued by the origins, particularly how each plant was used by indigenous populations. I poured over writings and research for hours.

Nothing else occupied my thoughts. My mind flooded with possibilities. *A violet-infused balm with ylang ylang. An orange blossom balm for second chakra. Should I follow the chakras, incorporate what I know from my year in yoga practices? Maybe I should keep it simple. I could do a line of chakra balms and a line of simple herbal oils.*

I began to share my excitement for my new inspirations when Alora, the guide from my year in yoga, sent me an email, fanning the flames. Alora had also stepped into new territory, leasing space in her local shopping center and opening a yoga studio with her daughter. She wanted to talk to me about creating a waterless and alcohol-free hand cleanser for the studio.

Ideas popped into my head the moment anyone opened their mouth. It was as if I was a direct channel to plant creativity. I knew exactly what I wanted to make. I had just purchased a new essential oil from a local wholesaler and in my research discovered an article about its effectiveness for just such a thing, when combined with lavender.

Alora offered to display my products for sale at her grand opening. I had blended a yoga mat spray for her and had many herbal infusions well underway. I needed to source bottles and labels and packaging. Convinced the universe was pulling me forcefully to my purpose, I didn't notice how happiness had subtly shifted to struggle as my plant-playing turned into branding and business.

I stopped surfing the wave, the gift of the island, the inner nectar of inspiration and creativity, and, assuming I had all the details I needed, I immaturely began to push these gifts out to the world. I had not yet my own understanding of the information I had been receiving, but in my haste to claim a purpose, I began to push back on the universe. I developed an agenda.

While I sourced sustainable packaging, I started infusing anything in my yard that I could identify. *How can people not know the multitude of benefits of the dandelion? If people knew this stuff, surely, we'd never spray it with weed killer again.* Ralph Waldo Emerson's words floated through my mind: *"A weed is a plant whose virtue is not yet known."*

An expanse of chickweed crept alongside my garden path. I had thought about pulling it out several times. It didn't bother me and I knew the benefits of it so I had left it to take over the path. Khali woke one morning with a swollen eye: half-closed, puffy and red. I wasn't sure what had happened overnight to cause the swelling.

She was fine otherwise, and I decided to give the chickweed and my Hawaiian chant a try. I pulled a handful of Stellaria Media, I called her Stella. I rinsed Stella in the kitchen sink and wadded her into a ball, placing it on Khali's closed eye while she lay on the couch, indulging me.

Khali received Stella therapy for no more than ten minutes, about as long as a four-year-old could lay still, watching cartoons through one eye. By lunch her eye was back to normal; the swelling and redness removed by Stella.

I played with plant after plant, ebullient from the essential oils, ecstatic from the herbs and deliriously delighted with the living allies. Senses heightened, I surfed the wave. I couldn't stop if I wanted to. The plants pulled me toward them. I would meet someone and within moments of talking with them, knew what plants or oils would best help their physical or emotional state. Every plant was a new friend, healer and teacher. I wanted to capitalize on this recent gift. I bottled up products for sale and advertised my open house.

So MUCH MEDICINE
   Healing strewn across the ground
   Wisdom of the plants

28

ITS A MATTER OF HEART

"I'm heading for the E.R," I told Steve on the phone. "Can you pick up the kids from school?"

The palpitations in my chest had grown severe. More than all my breathwork and meditative tools could handle. Fear's grip reached for me and I could no longer talk my way out of the need for medical attention.

I nearly passed out while bending over to pick up the watering can that morning. I found it difficult to catch my breath, and I couldn't tolerate the repeated shots to my chest anymore. Something was not right and whatever it was, was not going away.

I pulled into the hospital parking lot and headed for the emergency room. One thing my spinal injury had shown me years earlier was how life as I knew it could be over in a second once I lost my ability to walk or move. Luckily, that immobility had lasted only thirty-three days and not a lifetime. Suddenly even *that* injury paled in comparison to the life I knew ending entirely if my heart so chose.

Fortunately, my wait wasn't long. A hospital attendant shuffled me into a special room just off the waiting room for an EKG. Apparently, they don't like you to have a heart attack in the waiting room. Probably bad for business.

"Fantastic," enthused the technician, "you are currently experiencing an episode so we can capture a record of it. Most people stop having episodes by the time they get here, and we are unable to capture it."

How awesome for me. As a rule, I tried not to be sarcastic in my conversations, but my inner voice never got that memo. *The palpitations hadn't let up in three days. Why would they stop now?* I was exhausted from the non-stop circus in my chest. At least the record of the event should lead to correct and immediate diagnosis.

I returned to the waiting room. I surveyed the sombre room, sending blessings to everyone. A man lay on a padded bench while his wife and adult children comforted him. From the conversation, I gathered that he was supposed to have seen his regular doctor for a follow up yet had neglected to do so and his condition had deteriorated quickly. His family was visibly worried about him even though he tried to elevate their mood and concern, joking about what he wanted for lunch.

A young girl who looked as if she had a good case of the flu, sat huddled in a chair complaining aloud of the wait and her discomfort. I couldn't help but feel as though she should be at home looking after her flu with some rest, fluids, whatever meds she chose, and a little fortitude and patience. The man maintained a calmer head and lighter disposition than the young girl, yet I was certain his condition was serious and warranted her reaction and hers, his. It seemed a stark comparison, the ways in which each handled their suffering.

I sat in a chair against the far wall where I could see the entire room. *A coat of paint would go along way to boosting the mood of this place.* I breathed and smiled. *I may as well provide a source of calm energy while I'm here.* I watched the staff as they came and went, fetching patients from the waiting room. I sent them blessings of fortitude, gratitude and humour. Every person waiting looked annoyed, scared, worried, angry, or a combination. Except for the man who I thought was most likely in the worst shape.

The emergency staff had their hands full with a shift of never-ending illnesses and injuries. I assigned myself the position of peaceful presence. Worried about my own condition, I had no intention of adding to the emotional burden of the already taxed staff.

"Stephanie Her... Herer..." a nurse attempted to call my name. I stood up quickly, saving her another attempt, and followed her behind the walls of the waiting room to an assessment room. A nurse met me on the other side of the blue curtain. With a quick wit, unlike any I'd encountered from the medical field, he took my blood pressure and heart rate and asked me questions about my condition. I felt more like an audience member invited onstage at a Vegas show than an emergency room patient. I was grateful for the comic relief.

The doctor came into the room, rather my curtain-partitioned portion of the room. How Anna would have loved to make fun of me that day. Perhaps the most handsome of all the handsome men I'd been fortunate to encounter, the doctor also proved more nurturing than the average doc. It was a running joke with Anna and I: the handsome men who showed up to help me.

"Of course, you'd get the good-looking one," I could hear her voice in my head.

The doctor read my EKG results. "Premature ventricular contractions, or PVCs. They're more common than people know. Most people with them never even realize they have the condition."

"How could no one feel this?" I said, slapping my hand over my heart. "It's like being kicked repeatedly in the chest by a horse." The sensation was similar to the uncomfortable yet reassuring kicks of a baby in the belly, except this baby was a tiny strong man using my heart as a punching bag, and it made uncomfortable look like an ice cream sundae, and nothing reassuring came from the blows. Following due diligence, the handsome doc sent me for chest x-rays and blood work.

I happened upon another lovely gentleman, my x-ray technician. It seemed whenever I maintained an awareness of a situation and chose to bring light and gratitude rather than struggle against it, the universe somehow rewarded me with kind encounters. The more gently I treated myself and others, the more gently I was treated. Perhaps the key to the elusive law of attraction resided there. I received what I needed by becoming the source of it for someone else. Only my intention had never been to garner these things for myself, simply to bring ease to others.

I returned to my assessment cubical and my bedside entertainer, the nurse. We traded chit chat about my cute purse for exchanges about the even cuter doctor. I can hear Steve saying, "I'm right here you know." His usual response to me talking about good-looking men in front of him. He knows it's my appreciation for beautiful men that drew me to him.

"I tell ya'," said the nurse, "this is one place I'm happy to work overtime. As long as it's with Dr. Foxy over there."

I'd never had a conversation about a man I found handsome, with another man that found him equally handsome, until then.

"Let's take some blood, honey, then I'll have you wait for your results in a chair in the hallway." He tied the blue elastic around my arm. "Trust me, the people-watching's better out there. If you've got to be stuck in Emerg, you might as well enjoy yourself."

He filled the last of the vials with my crimson life force and taped a cotton ball to my arm. I thanked him and grabbed my things. I took one of the six seats in the hall and relaxed into the chair.

A young girl, no more than twenty, sat next to me, wringing her hands out in distress. I struck up a conversation with her.

"Where are you from?' I asked.

"Vancouver," she replied in a soft voice. "I'm just visiting for the weekend. I go to University there. So does my boyfriend. I'm eight weeks pregnant and I keep bleeding."

"Well it's good that you've come to the hospital to get it checked out," I said. "Often these things are nothing, but it's best to see a doctor."

"We never meant to get pregnant."

"No?"

"I want to have the baby and be with him, but... I'm afraid what his parents might think."

"Oh, why is that? Do you not get along with them?"

"He's Arab. His family doesn't know about me or the baby."

I suddenly felt as if my trip to the ER had nothing to do with me and everything to do with the people I encountered. The young girl was alone, and I was an ear and a shoulder for her. I didn't have a good feeling about the outcome with her boyfriend, his family, and their secret relationship and baby, but it was none of my business. All I could do was offer the wisest words I could find at the time.

Bear energy rose in me: protective and fierce. "Make decisions for you," I said. "Make choices that help you feel supported. Do what you know is right for you and ask for help if you need it. Do you have family?"

"I haven't seen my dad since I moved away from home."

"Do you have a good relationship with him?"

"Oh, yes, it's good," she smiled.

"You need to call him. Let him know what's going on so he can support you." This was a time for family. She needed someone in her corner. "I'm sure the baby will be okay," I reassured her, "and if for some reason it's not, *you* will be okay."

I felt a strong need to reinforce to her that no matter what happened, she would be alright. Like she needed that seed planted deep inside her as I had as a young girl. The words that mysteriously came to me one day in my room during a trying time, as if floating through the air, "No matter what happens, things will always work out."

Dr. Handsome returned with my test results. He gave me a clean bill of health. Aside from the dizziness, inability to catch my breath, and onslaught of right hooks from my heart, I was the poster child for perfect health. Due to my nearly-nonexistent cholesterol levels, there was no need for concern over the PVCs. The doctor was generous with his assurances that nothing bad was going to happen, and he ordered further tests to help put me at ease. It seemed a bit of *paying it forward* from the exchange that had just happened between me and the young girl.

I passed the subsequent heart tests with flying colours, although it was embarrassing to quit the treadmill stress test thirteen minutes into the fifteen-minute test. My fitness level could handle the test, but my heart's crazy dance kept the blood from pumping through my body at the required rate. My arms became numb and dizziness forced me to choose safety over ego.

How can a fit, young woman, and previous personal trainer, nearly pass out during a stress test and have nothing wrong? I knew the events had something to do with the foray into plants, but I'd examined all the angles, except the ones I denied to myself. I researched all the plants I worked with for any common side effects. I stopped working with them for a period to see if the symptoms went away.

The truth was, the symptoms worsened every time I struggled with making the plants my business. When I played with the plants for my own personal and creative satisfaction and exploration, life was good. When I slaved for hours over finding the perfect packaging, labelling, website content, and marketing and delivery of the *products*, life became a struggle which revealed itself through my heart.

The plants were a gift and they taught me valuable lessons, one of which was that not everything is meant to be made into a business. I sought so hard for my purpose, my unique contribution, that every time I happened upon something that I loved and received healing or joy from, I convinced myself that was my purpose and I had only to figure out how to sell it to others. I was so determined to find my purpose, I made *everything* my purpose.

I loved learning about and making balms and oils, and they soothed my body and soul. Somehow, I couldn't see that perhaps that was their only purpose: to soothe me. A wave of obsession would wash over me with each new inspiration, and I would search and source ways to make it my life's work. I hadn't yet learned to listen to the struggle.

Once the sonogram came back showing a structurally healthy heart, I knew I needed to tune in to what my heart was telling me. The plants had been for *me*, to learn from and perhaps share that learning with others, but never to package up and sell. How awesome to realize once again I'd jumped into something, put all my resources behind it, convinced everyone else this was it, only to lose momentum and have to back out gracefully.

Another failure under my belt, my ego wouldn't let me quit altogether. I continued to fill orders but immediately discontinued promoting my business of plants. I had several studios stocking my oils and over the following six months I began to pull out of the business.

The pull of the plants themselves, however, had become an addiction, and I continued to receive dreams of plants and synchronicities that led to discovering and working with new plant teachers. I just couldn't understand the purpose of it all if not to be *my* purpose. My impatience to find my way in the world, from which I would make my livelihood, distracted me from remembering I was still in school.

Another lost purpose and a storage room filled with packaging and supplies, the weight of the wasted investment of my time and money was still considerably less than the weight lifted off my heart upon my decision to let it all go. I slowly withdrew my outward expansion of the business, offering more intimate open-house events for my clients and keeping up the appearance of business as usual. It wasn't all a façade. I was as in love with the plants as ever, just not with the business.

I'd experienced enough failures in the past that I believed my heart knew I would exhaust myself in order to make the plant business a success. The fear of failure and my determination to beat it would stronghold me along a path I was never meant to walk. The further I pushed down that path, the more intense the palpitations. When I let go of the need to succeed, the palpitations slowly decreased in frequency. I had to live with the failure of the business, but I chose to pay that price over the failure of my health. I decided the ego was easier to heal than the heart.

TOO MUCH ENERGY
expended but not reclaimed
Temper mind with heart

29

PACKAGING UP MY FAILURE

I stood in my storage room, saddened by the waste. *What am I going to do with all these herbs?* Three walls of shelves held everything from organic calendula blossoms to St. John's wort powder, beeswax to Fair Trade shea butter, ylang ylang essential oil to aloe vera gel, and more.

I picked up a bottle of lavender hydrosol and twisted off the cap for a deep draw of the plant water's aroma. I had sourced it from a small farm owned by a shaman. He recited mantra to his lavender while it grew, and harvested it biodynamically: by the moon's phases. *Man, I love this stuff.*

I had to figure out what to do with a room-full of plant medicine. I didn't want it to go to waste but who would be interested in it? *I guess, worst-case scenario, I'll feed it back to the land. Sure be nice if someone loved it as much as I do.*

The thing about change is that when it's time, it's time. And I'm all in. I carried every package of petals, every bottle of essential oil, every flat of fair trade butter, and every powder, liquid, and container from the storage room out into my open studio. I placed it all on the floor.

There's something clarifying that comes from seeing what you've accumulated all laid out before you. *I've taken too much.* Four-hundred square feet of studio and there was not even enough room for me to sit on the floor.

I lowered my head. *Shit.* Tears pooled in the corners of my eyes. *I'm sorry.* Shame and guilt swam up from inside me. I drew a cleansing breath and let them go. Lesson learned.

Famished, I left the studio filled with failing and forgiveness. I grabbed a snack and then headed outside to enjoy it in the sun. I was nearly finished when a neighbour waved hello.

"How are you?" I asked, walking over to the fence that sided the community walking path.

"Well, hello, beautiful," she sang in her Iranian accent. It was years earlier –I tell the story in *An Accidental Awakening*– that this lovely neighbour introduced me to my reiki friend, Sophie.

We shared an over-the-fence hug as she continued. "What is happening with you? Are you still doing the plants?"

"Sadly, no," I replied. " And now I have a studio filled with herbs and essential oils. I have no idea what to do with them." I popped my last bite of lunch into my mouth.

"Oh! You need to talk to my friend. She gives the most amazing treatments for the face and the energy works. She lives just across the road, you know... the coulee road. She is finishing her studies of herbalism and wants to make her own healing products."

"Really?"

"Yes!" Her little dog began pulling at the leash. "I will email you her phone number when I get home."

"That would be fantastic. Thank you." I gave her another

hug before her dog pulled her up the path toward her house.

I headed back inside and opened my laptop. It was only minutes before her email arrived in my inbox. *Might as well.* I picked up the phone and dialled.

Within mere hours, we were sitting on the studio floor, packages of herbs in our laps to make room, talking for hours about all-things herbal, metaphysical and spiritual. This new acquaintance shared many of my passions. With long raven hair and glowing freckled skin, she exuded the energy of a medicine woman.

We finally got down to business. "I only took out $250 from the machine," she said. "I had no idea that you had so many herbs."

"It's yours," I replied. "Take it all. I need to know that someone is making good use of all of this plant energy."

With the exception of the packaging materials, I helped her load the rest of my inventory into her vehicle. It was now dark. It took the two of us many trips up and down the sandstone path. The cold stones woke my bare feet. I finally hugged her goodbye and returned down the path to my studio. I stood in the opening. Only bottles and containers remained.

"MYTH IS RISING all over the world. Myth gives us the coding in the story of ourselves, rip-large, as the hero and heroine of a thousand faces."[1]

I stacked violet glass balm containers on the shelf as Dr. Jean Houston's voice reverberated through my laptop speakers.

"This is the time. We are the people. If not now, when? If

not you, who?" Dr. Houston's words travelled across my skin, leaving goosebumps in their wake — though they made the road to my purpose no clearer, only more urgent.

"In all the great stories, the wounding was the entrance to the sacred. It was through the wounding that the depths could rise."

I wrapped a large elastic around a dozen green plastic massage oil bottles while her words continued to excite the very molecules of my being. The mundane work of organizing the remains of my herbal endeavour felt much less mundane. I worked quickly to keep up with both my sorting and her words.

I wasn't familiar with Dr. Houston and had a tough time maintaining pace with the call. She spoke quickly and passionately and I half paid attention as I moved back and forth between the studio and the storage room, organizing the hundreds of empty bottles, containers, and fair-trade packaging, hand-made from banana leaf and wild grass fibres.

"Call in the Master of what it is you wish to learn," she guided listeners through an exercise.

Normally I would have jumped at the opportunity for exploration of the inner world, but I had much to do and just enough motivation to do it. I skipped the exercise and kept banding and boxing while Dr. Houston shared the antidote to educational atrophy. Her words punctuated the soundtrack of my failed venture while simultaneously seeding me with new possibilities.

At the end of the talk, Jean offered an opportunity to study with her in an online community. I signed up. As I closed the storage room door on my plant business, another classroom door opened.

. . .

ENDINGS, beginnings
   Linear is deceiving
   All comes full circle

30

RELEASE FEAR

"Stop seeking."

I was only minutes into the kundalini yoga kriya practice when he whispered to me. I know because the burn had not yet begun in my shoulders. I heard the words clearly yet continued to raise my arms in sync with the chant.

I had committed to the forty-day practice intended to "release fear and become a conscious leader". *One does not simply stop.* I kneeled on the floor of the studio with my heels directly under my butt, arms extended forward. I breathed and bowed in time with the music and the mantra. It wasn't the first forty-day Global Sadhana I'd participated in through *Spirit Voyage* but it was my favourite so far. "Aadays Tisai Aadays..." the music seduced my soul and coerced my arms to continue even though I knew the intense burning in my shoulders would soon begin.

On the first day of practice, I had completed the full thirty minutes, so I knew its behaviour. Once I passed a certain point, burning would give way to breakthrough. I assumed it was a release of endorphins or other chemicals coursing through my body, akin to a runner's high, only more blissful and vast: a yogini's high.

I had recalled Dr. Houston's exercise from her webinar: calling in the master of what you wish to learn. I had taken a brief moment as I set up for my practice, asking the master of yoga to come teach me. In my mind I had seen yoga blocks and straps in a studio. I anticipated learning about yoga from a great yogi perhaps.

I don't recall how many days I was into the forty-day practice. Not many. Not even a week. Eyes nearly closed, focused on the tip of my nose, spine long and straight, I chanted in a melodic trance, "...Aad Aneel Anaad Anaahat Jug Jug Ayko Vays." My body firm and straight, my spirit sank into the beauty of the mantra and the music. I had exactly enough time to do my practice and get to school to pick up Khali, after a brief stop at the grocery store. Committed to my practice, I ignored the whisper.

"Stop seeking!" commanded the voice and my arms dropped to my lap as if someone had pushed them down. Snatam Kaur's voice continued to sing the practice from my laptop as if nothing had happened.

A man stood in front of the most magnificent tree. It's trunk sturdy and deeply-rooted, it's leafy canopy far-reaching. He moved aside, motioning with his hand for me to sit in his spot at its base. Buddha was offering me his place at the base of the Bodhi tree.

I began to cry. Stupid girl. I had assumed the master of yoga would teach me about asanas and give me the knowledge to teach others. I had not considered this great teacher and master. My head fell to my chest as my eyes filled with tears and my heart with humility.

"Remember the love you glimpsed at the cathedral in Sedona?" he asked. The image I saw that day, more than six months earlier, flooded me. As Jesus had stood before me, I felt only a moment of a depth of love I thought I'd never known, and yet somehow knew I'd once known it well. It was a taste of the sweetest nectar. A drop of something so powerful, my state at the time – and perhaps my human form — could not have handled more. I felt that if I'd stayed in the love, the full force of it, I'd have died that day, unable to hold its brilliance. Strange, I know, but there it is.

I began to cry as I remembered feeling the love, feeling I did not deserve it, wishing I could hold it, know it, and keep it. Mary had stepped in quickly to comfort me: a gentle filter of the love. I had felt my body calm upon her appearance, the feeling of pending dissolution of my physical self ceased in that moment.

"More of that love is coming to you," Buddha continued, and I cried harder. He spoke and his words reached me, but I was left with little memory of the rest of the conversation. I bawled as I sat on my heels, still in position from my practice. My tears emptied for what felt like hours, perhaps days, as his words continued.

The music stopped, pulling me from my trance and my tears. Nearly thirty minutes had passed, which suddenly felt like a moment, and I needed to leave right away to pick up groceries and Khali. I asked, rather, begged him to stay with me. He said he is always in my heart. I opened my eyes and tried to move my body. My mind was blank yet clear. I felt cried-out: emptied of whatever existed in me before.

My weakened body was slow to respond to my desire to stand: like I'd been away from the world. Thoughts ceased to exist in my mind, devoid of busy-ness. My body needed to remember how to move and it would not be rushed or pushed. I found my feet and stood: dreamy yet clear:

exhausted and content as if I'd mourned a great loss yet grateful to receive a great love.

I put on my shoes and drove to the store. I wanted only two things: not to talk or be spoken to, and to know that he was still with me. I didn't want anything to shear the silence nor the feeling of emptiness. I spoke only to ask silently of my heart, "Are you still with me?"

"Yes," he replied, as strong and clear as I had heard him in the studio.

I pulled a shopping cart from the entrance of the store and pushed it through the sliding doors. Another shopper's cart blocked me from continuing. I had no thought about it, no reaction or response. I stood, content to wait in my state of emptiness. A man quickly appeared, fetching the cart.

"I am sorry," he said.

Not wanting to interrupt my empty state with words yet not wishing to be rude, I casually offered, "No worries," and began to move around his cart. He stopped and looked directly at me, drawing my gaze from my cart to his face.

"No," he continued slow and deliberate, "I apologize."

His words sank into my soul. It was as if he was apologizing for everything. For all suffering and struggle in my life. Like he came only to give me that message and comfort. I looked deeply into his eyes. He was East Indian, with warm brown eyes and dark, shoulder-length hair. He was older than me, yet his skin glowed with youth. I felt as if I looked into the eyes of Yogananda Paramahansa.

I smiled at him and my body began to move away but not before I glanced into his cart. I don't know why. It was empty except for one item in the top basket: one bunch of red flowers, so vibrant in colour they stood out as if the rest of the world was in black and white, save for me, the apologetic fellow, and the flowers. Either roses or tulips, I don't recall — simply red and magnificent. It was as if the whole universe had become available to me.

I headed to preschool, still in my state of emptiness. This was not an emptiness by choice or something I had to work at or employ meditative tools to maintain. This was a state of having nothing inside me, no words, thoughts, no emotions. I felt only spacious and raw from the experience of emptying. Raw from the crying and the loss. I entered the school and immediately a woman approached me to chat.

Normally I gathered Khali and left without conversation, not knowing the other parents. For some strange reason, a woman with whom I'd never spoken, a petit and beautiful East Indian woman who always dressed well in slacks or skirts with patent black leather heels and a dress coat, came over and struck a lively conversation. I knew only how well she dressed and how patient she was with the children she picked up for her after-school care program, waiting for them to gather their things and put on their outdoor shoes.

I was thankful she had much to say, as I wanted to say nothing and her generous stream of words left me only enough room to smile, nod and confirm her from time to time. My whole body vibrated, even the space outside my body. I listened to her, to what she had to say. I heard every word and felt no need to offer any great response, insight, opinion, or present myself in any manner.

I had no manner, just an empty shell, tender on the inside. I simply heard her as she spoke about the struggles with the children in her program and how she strived to take care of their challenges and needs. It seemed to satisfy her as she looked content with our exchange.

"You have a wonderful day," she concluded and turned to collect the kids. How fortunate they were to have her care for them.

I brought Khali home, fed her lunch and conducted the day as usual, with two main differences: the raw emptiness of a new start lingered, and every few moments I repeated the question, "Are you still here?"

"Yes," came the response yet I felt the strength of the voice lessening in my ears.

We headed to Michael's school to pick him up. Usually I stood around talking to my dear friend Tanya for over an hour while the kids played. It was like a playdate for Moms. I looked forward to chatting with her each day. Not this day.

Michael crossed the field and I motioned to him so he knew where I was. I remained on the outskirts of the school-yard, at the furthest and least-used playground, perched on the branch of a tree. The spring sun warmed my face and the firm tree trunk supported my spine. I glimpsed Tanya at the other playground, talking to another friend of ours. I leaned further into the tree, hoping she would not see me but willing to visit with my friend should she approach.

"Are you still here?" I asked again, desperately afraid he would leave me and I would no longer hear his voice.

"Yes," he replied again, his voice fainter as my thoughts and feelings made their slow return. Slow enough that I lingered over an hour in silence with the sun and the tree and the vivid memory of the day's gifts. It saddened me to return to life without his voice, to be unable to hear him clearly. But I'd been given a precious treasure and the ability to return to life with the memory of its beauty.

The next day Tanya told me she had seen me at the school, yet I had appeared to be in some sort of bubble, she said, and she knew I didn't want to be disturbed. She had honoured that. I thanked her, telling her only that something very special and powerful had happened to me: a gift for which I was wholly grateful.

I didn't continue with the Global Sadhana, although to this day, listening to Snatam Kaur sing the enchanted mantra re-ignites the memory contained within my cells. I didn't continue because the mantra fulfilled its purpose. It united me with the master I sought and the master's words, "Stop seeking."

FOR WHAT DO YOU SEARCH?

To seek purpose, search not what
Search instead for whom

31

INTERIM PROFESSOR

J ean's course wasn't a short one. I committed to six months of study with Dr. Houston. I dove into the course and the online community. At first, I reserved opinion, unwilling to share personal information on the site. Others seemed comfortable exposing themselves. It was my year in yoga's second chakra gathering all over again: TMI. *Ugh*! I gradually reached out and commented on the page. My words met replies of support and encouragement. The community contained many women struggling with one issue or another: health, emotional pain, death of a loved one or divorce. Many sought their purpose as diligently as I. Most were quick to offer a kind remark or commiserate to extend a connection.

I rarely made the live online sessions, instead, listening to the recording the following day. I stretched my body into poses on my yoga mat, creating space for new content. I could only digest half of a call at once. Jean's passionate speech and provocative thoughts dropped me to my knees in an effort to get down on paper the insights and ah-ha moments that flowed through my body and mind.

Warrior I to Warrior II: I funneled her wisdom through my hips. Warrior II windmill through Downdog: my flow refined her ideas until they crystallized into methods I could apply in my life. I tasted my desire to write about my year in yoga. I smelled my yearning to be of benefit to others. I heard the sound of the earth healing. I was becoming that possible human of whom Jean spoke.

"Just try Jean's exercises first," I said to my computer while lying in Savasana. "Do the work for yourself. Don't expect her to fix it for you." I understood others in the course community struggled with personal issues, but I had little patience with the questions they posed at the end of the lessons. I skipped past the Q&A parts of the recordings after the first couple.

I scrolled through the comments and read the poetic postings of a particularly outspoken and artistic woman on the community site in a group I'd joined for writers. The others responded with immense support. I decided to post a page from my own writing, from the year in yoga. It was the first time I had put my story out for consumption, scrutiny, and judgment. My writing on a sweet site called *Cowbird* had consisted of stand-alone pieces, musings, most of which came to me with little struggle, effort or thought. My year in yoga story was a more complicated work.

I pressed *post*. My mind twisted with scenarios. *What if no one comments because it sucks. What if no one comments because I'm not like the others: I'm not vulnerable or emotional enough to warrant inclusion. What if no one comments because I've been looking down my nose at them as they posed their questions to Jean.*

Several supportive responses followed my post, the most supportive of which came from the poet herself. She commented on how she looked forward to further postings and following the arc of the story. *Whew*. I made it through preliminary exposure only to realize I had little idea of my own craft. Story arc was a long-lost term from my high school days. *How can I write a book, how can this be my great work, if I don't even know my own art?*

I felt like I'd put the cart before the horse. The story came first. Learning how to write it came later. As odd as that felt, unqualified to write my own story, I imagined being the most skilled writer without a story to tell: equally excruciating. Thanks to the group support, I'd survived the first step while I inched my way toward confidence in my story.

I stayed with Jean's course the entire six months, even through the summer: squeezing time on my mat in between filling the blow-up kiddie pool, watermelon breaks, farmers' market excursions and trips to Grandma's house. I fell off during the final three weeks. I skipped two of the lessons in order to listen to the final one and feel as though I finished alongside the course community.

Six months had flown by and I felt enthusiasm for the possible, though I had no idea where to aim that enthusiasm. I felt like an evolutionary. Not sure what to evolve, my attention returned to writing.

I HAVE NOT LEFT you
  I am refocusing you
  Soon you'll understand

32

PIE IN THE SKY

M y eyes scanned the pages of my journal marked *2009*. I had begun journaling during my year in yoga: mainly in point form or long-winded rants. The practices during that year had cracked something open in me. The more I meditated, the more I moved my body through asana or walked in nature, the harder the writing bug bit me

Initially, I processed the often-bizarre rituals of that year in yoga through my pen. As the year had continued, however, great moments of clarity, insight, or spiritual inspiration sparked the flow of ink. What started as conversations with myself soon morphed into dialogue with the cosmos. Layers upon layers of *realities* revealed themselves to me. If I couldn't make sense of them, at least I could document them for later — perhaps for others who struggled with issues of spiritual awakening in the midst of injury, mother-hood and mid-life.

I criticized my earlier writing as I flipped through the pages: my immaturity and self-absorption. It was exhausting to follow me from one end of the pendulum – defending one point of view – to the other, as my mind tried to tie the events in my life into one neat little bow. Most often I couldn't explain the experiences and in trying to do so, tangled myself up in yet another position. Writing my thoughts may have helped me at the time but reading them gave me a headache. *How did I get through a day with that much noise in my head?*

I hired a local editor. Although wordy, to me, my musings felt like gold thread woven across the mind's blank page. But what would a professional think of my *treasure*? Hopefulness turned heartbreak when I read the first pages of her comments. "Needs substantial work. You are no longer allowed to use the following 25 words, beginning with the word *beautiful*." Apparently, my brain had erroneously convinced me I could write.

How can I have such a drive to write yet suck at it? I sat at my laptop, reviewing her notes and wondering where to begin. *What a mess. Molding the book into something tangible is going to be impossible. If only someone was paying me to write or had an interest in it, I'd have a reason to keep writing and some sort of deadline to aim for.* I needed the motivation to continue.

I opened a new tab and clicked on Facebook. I scrolled the posts. *Wait a minute.* I backed up the feed. Hay House posted an invitation for writers to submit their work, with one to be awarded a publishing contract.

"This is it!" I yelled to no one in particular in my kitchen. I like to think there is always a full house of supporters and friends hanging out with me. They laugh at all my jokes. It beats the cat giving me that blank stare.

The contest deadline was three weeks away. *Perfect.* I had

asked for a deadline and the universe had just handed me one. I got to work, determined to sew together the pieces I had written over the year in yoga into one seamless story. I had the feedback to work with and motivation to finish it, which, at that stage of the game, was all I wanted to do: finish it and be done.

NEARLY THREE WEEKS later I had pulled together much of the pieces of my year. It looked a lot like the dress I sewed in Grade 10 Home Ec: one sleeve considerably longer than the other and an unravelling hem. There was no way I could hand in some slapped together rush job to Hay House.

"Aaaaargghh!" I slammed my laptop shut and took Khali outside to play at the playground. It was a stunning day – late summer, deep blue sky, leaves changing – all the time I had spent indoors, at my laptop, plugging away at the book while my children grew up. I was wasting my life and theirs. I threw my hands up to the endless azure sky and cried, "Grandfather Sky, I'm done. Tell me what to do. Either burn it or finish it, I don't care. Either way. I just need it to end."

Honestly burning it held great appeal. I could see a ritual with chanting, candles, and a completion to my year in yoga. I needed to be set free. Torching the source of my torture seemed the simplest way out.

I returned to the house with Khali and checked my email. I had received one from Maestro Path, the platform that hosted Jean Houston's online course, but it had nothing to do with Jean's course. The subject line read "Ready to write your book?"

. . .

THERE'S no need to yell
  Make certain of your request
  Ask for what you want

33

GUEST LECTURER

I felt awkward asking Steve if he minded watching the kids while I listened to a free call about writing my book. I imagined he thought I was being led down the garden path while someone fed me a sales pitch akin to buying encyclopedias. I had to make the call, after all, I had asked for it. *Birth Your Book: From Inspiration to Published Author* – Grandfather Sky couldn't have been clearer than that. I assumed the speaker would be an English professor-type: male, with old school teachings about the format and foundation of writing.

I closed the office doors and dialed the call-in number provided in the email confirmation. A woman introduced the speaker, Lisa Tener, book writing coach. A bright, crisp, cheerful female voice welcomed us all and thanked us for joining her. Lisa invited a recent participant in her book writing course to speak about her experience of landing a top agent. An agent. That seemed like a whole other world to me. I simply wanted to put the pieces of my life scrawled on pages of loose-leaf and journals into a story with a beginning, middle, and end.

Lisa said she was going to share five keys to writing our books during the call. She mentioned that the end of the call would include how to attract a six-figure book deal. I felt so far from that place, in mind, intention, and writing. I needed someone to help me complete my book, period. Perhaps the call was more of a sales pitch than I'd hoped.

"Feel your feet grounded on the floor and allow your spine to gently straighten, comfortably... as you breathe out, release any tension you feel from the day..." Lisa's voice guided us through an opening visualization to access inner wisdom about our books. *Damn, this is my girl. She speaks my language.* Clearly Grandfather Sky had my back and wanted to make sure I didn't doubt the synchronicity of my request and the call.

I listened and participated in the exercises. Inspiration mounted as I answered questions on paper about my book and why I was writing it. Lisa asked questions I had never considered asking myself. As I dug around inside me for the answers, my passion swelled to create a great book. Then she got to the sales pitch and it was game over for me.

Her eight-week program to complete my book was exactly what I needed, not too long, not too intense, doable. Her price was more than I could even consider pitching to Steve. He already thought my writing was a hobby I entertained.

I ran my own business, but I'd stopped teaching my regular yoga classes to accommodate the herbal products and had spent most of my money on supplies. My business bank account didn't have the money to cover the course. At home, with two kids, not generating an income, I was not about to ask Steve if I could put us further in debt for my writing. I had already failed at the herbal product business, although admitting that to myself or anyone else hadn't happened yet. I didn't need to fail at yet another expensive investment of my time, money and energy.

I told Steve about Lisa, how she spoke my language and offered great advice on the call, then revealed the cost of the course, preempting the figure with, "It was a lot more than I'd thought." I went to bed, perplexed by the day's events. I had become fed up enough to want to burn my work, vulnerable enough to ask for help from the universe, surprised and delighted by the response, and then baffled by the commitment required.

The entire next day I thought about the events, the coincidence, the perfect fit of Lisa with me, and the possibility of completing my book and that it could actually be good, not just done. The follow-up email came, offering the discount if I signed up by Friday. Lisa had also mentioned during the call that she was happy to have a private conversation with anyone to decide if working with her was a good fit. I wanted to call her. *What would I say: I desperately want to take your course but am too terrified to ask my husband for the money to justify writing a book? How professional. And sad.*

I thought about it for two days. Friday morning came, the registration deadline for the course. I summoned the courage to call Lisa. I didn't know what I was going to say. I decided to make the call and allow the words to emerge during our conversation. I sat on the front step in the sun and explained to Lisa the compelling nature of my book and the inability to build an equally compelling case to sell my husband. I told her it was difficult to ask for such an amount when finishing the book was not meant to attract the six-figure deal but simply give me peace of mind of completion.

Truth be told, I hadn't the confidence in either my writing abilities nor the story to actually place value on my writing. My heart and gut aligned on my desire to write a book. My head, however, was the hold-out. I didn't believe in me. Not enough to take a leap of faith that required pre-payment.

Lisa didn't try to sell me on her course, instead, she guided me through her *Meet Your Muse* visualization to ask my muse whether the class was an optimal way for me to write my book and, if so, where I could find the money to cover the cost of the course. She led me through the visual-ization, step by step. I followed along in the warmth of the sun on my front step. It was easy to drop into the guided meditation in the location of my usual daily practice. Deeper inward I dove.

"Now see your Muse standing in the doorway," Lisa said.

I gasped aloud at what I saw. In my mind's eye, I stood face to face with the warm smile and kind eyes of the guide I had met during my first guided meditation led by my friend Sophie two years earlier. I had forgotten about this guide and the many inner trips to seek his advice about my life's purpose.

I had forgotten about the images and information he showed me during that initial session on Sophie's treatment table and then on my own over the subsequent weeks. I had forgotten about the wall of books for me to write and the pens he kept handing me to write with. I cried with both delight in our reunion and sadness in my forgetfulness.

After a long hug and warm exchange, I asked my muse the question, "Is Lisa's program right for me at this time?"

"Yes," came his response.

"Then where am I to find the money to pay for it?"

My muse showed me the change dish on the window ledge of my office. I laughed. Surely, I didn't have enough change in there to cover the cost.

It wasn't about the change, though. I had put the dish

there to collect all the coins lying around the house. My muse was telling me the money I needed was spread around the house too. I had a hard time believing the amount I needed was scattered about my home, but I told Lisa it was worth a try and set out to see what I could find. She extended the deadline for the discounted rate to Monday. I had until the end of the weekend to follow the trail of coins.

I started with the client cheques I had yet to deposit, not nearly enough but a start. There was a pile of mail I hadn't gotten around to opening. I opened an envelope from the government which I figured was a monthly "baby bonus" cheque of $100 that we receive in Canada. I thought that was at least something. I opened it to find a reassessment on my corporate taxes in the amount of $250. *Cool!*

There was a second government envelope, I knew that one would be the $100 cheque. I opened it to find a second refund, $900! *What*? I headed to the bank to make my various deposits and discovered there was more in my corporate account than I remembered. My muse had been right and in one day I found a windfall of money just laying around. The best part: it was all corporate money and not only provided me with an investment in my work but also didn't require approval from Steve.

Still, I had begun to feel the book held greater potential, especially after my reunion with my guide and the ensuing cash-fall, and I wanted Steve's support to help me realize it. When he returned home from work, I sat down with him. I couldn't stop smiling and he already knew whatever I was about to ask him for was beyond him saying no. He knew me and knew I had made up my mind about something. Suddenly, amazed by Grandfather Sky, inspired by Lisa, and funded by, apparently the government, and several clients, I had unlimited ability to build a compelling case to write my book.

"I want to finish something in my life. I want to bring something to completion," I started to explain to Steve. "I didn't attend my high school graduation, I was in Quebec on a bursary to study French. I didn't complete either of my post-secondary fields. I want to finish something. I want to succeed at bringing one thing to completion."

I needed to do it for me. Whether it was published or not, read or not, I wasn't thinking that far ahead. I just wanted to not fail at this one thing. The most personal, challenging, vulnerable, and consuming task I'd ever undertaken, and I needed to prove to myself that I could succeed.

I couldn't throw a grad cap up in the air or receive a diploma from a professor in front of fellow students and proud family — not that I couldn't go back to school, but I had little insight as to what would compel me toward years of study in my forties — but I *could* know that I didn't waste my potential.

What I didn't realize at the time was that my life lesson was not solely about completion, but about getting all the information and staying on purpose. I had spent my life rushing toward the finish line. I had left my first Diploma program after year one, my second as well. I always had a reason or an excuse. I failed time and again for two reasons: I wasn't patient enough to wait for what was seeking me, to find me, and I hadn't stopped to hear my heart.

I called Lisa right away to share the incredible story of the found finances. I pulled up her website and registered for the course, poised to pay. *Wait a minute. This is a lot of money. You know what I could do with this money? Once I hit the pay button, my bank account returns to zero. I could use this for something else. Many things.*

Thankfully the moment was brief. I knew the money came for the sole purpose of funding the book. You don't invite the muse into your life and then say, *Nah*. I'd learned to trust my intuition during my year in yoga. I was not about to look that gift horse in the mouth. I clicked the payment button. It was the biggest investment I had made in myself in a long time, perhaps ever. It would reach far beyond financial. It would prove to be the greatest investment of time, energy, trust, belief, courage, creativity, emotional fortitude, and sheer will that I had ever made.

Maybe we're too wound up in bringing things to completion — our understanding of completion. Maybe nature has a different understanding. Maybe each of our nature's has its own natural completion. Perhaps my struggle with finishing something simply required me to understand my nature. Maybe I was more of a fire starter, an embracer of change, a sampler, a taster, a tester, a forager, an explorer. Perhaps it was okay to quit. Maybe my lessons resided in letting go. I loved the feeling of quitting something. Truth be told, my ego, my conditioning, hated raising the flag of defeat and could mine all sorts of gems of excuses to keep from declaring a loss. But my heart, oh my heart loved the relief of just dropping something that I no longer held any love for.

R*UMI* W*ROTE* *it well*
> *Beyond right and wrongdoing*
> *there's indeed a field*

34

LIFE IS A CIRCLE

I walked the hill to my sacred place. It had been months since I'd visited, consumed with my writing. I wanted to share my progress with the hill and the woman in deerskin and red. My fingertips greeted the long grasses as I walked. I bowed my head at the broken barbed wire gate and silently requested permission to enter. The hill warmly greeted me, like an old relative, happy to see me.

I took only a few steps inside the wire perimeter when I saw it. *No. No. Not here. Who did this? Not here. Of all places, not here!*

The wild grasses were gone: Harebells and brown-eyed Susans ripped from their soil. Deep trenches dug into the hill's skin. The logs I once perched upon in meditation were now a ramp. Neighbourhood kids. They had torn up my sacred place to use for their bike trails.

My clenched fists squeezed tears from my eyes as options flew across my mind. *Do I report it to the community association? Do I wait and identify the kids? Do I call the city? Do I organize remediation? Do I let my anger loose on those who cannot see her?*

My heart fell along with my tears and I walked away from the destruction toward the mountains. I stood, head hung, deflated. *How can they not see the beauty and the magic of this place? How do they not feel it?*

Through my tears I saw blue. Blurred but blue. I wiped my eyes and looked again. There, amid the remaining matted grasses was a lone harebell. I bent down to see her more clearly. Next to her grew a crocus. One purple prairie crocus. The first sign of spring.

"That's not possible," I told her. "I mean, is it even possible for you to bloom now? It's October."

I was so lost in the moment that I almost didn't hear the woman approach. I had never met another person at my site. Suddenly, it appeared to be a community hot spot. I quickly wiped my face and stood up to greet her.

She was an older woman in a purple jacket. I shared the crocus with her. She seemed as pleased and astounded as I. She said she lived in the seniors' condos. She had traversed quite a distance to get from her home to the hilltop. I walked her back down the hill, around Two-toed Pond, across the road and back up the other side to the main walking path. I don't know why she was there… at that exact moment at my sacred place. A comfort? A kindred spirit? A distraction from my grief? Why had Spirit placed her there at that time?

THE NEXT DAY, I picked through my collection of crystals, looking for the right one to leave as an offering for the crocus. I slipped into my shoes and out the back door. I headed for my hill.

Sadness returned when I reached the wire gate and once

again saw the destruction of my sacred place. I sniffed back tears and bee-lined for the crocus. Holding the crystal in both hands close to my heart, I infused the stone with a swell of gratitude, "If you can find the strength to bloom in October, then I can find the strength to believe humanity will see you again." I tucked it under the grasses at the feet of the crocus. "I love you and I thank you." My personal prayer sealed my offering.

Something moved behind me. I spun around to *see* a being emerge from the hilltop: first her head and torso, then her considerable wings. She pulled her knees into her chest for warmth. Her tousled blond hair fell over her shoulders. Her feet were bare, and she wore a white sheath of a dress.

The experience mimicked the visions of the Elder woman, but the energy was very different. This was an earth angel. I knew it because I felt it. One can't simply explain these things. The strange part was that she was sad. I felt that too. She wasn't ethereal and joyful. She was definitely grace. But she was sad, bordering on disappointed.

Tears of gratitude streamed down my face as she transmitted her story to me. This was her hill. This was her sacred place. She once walked it freely, in conversation with the trees, the animals and even the people who had known her language. But those people stopped coming. Other people came. They didn't know her language. She crawled into the hill to sleep an infinite sleep.

"You're blessing woke me." It had been the first time someone had acknowledged her — through her precious hillside extension — in a very long time. But I could see that she was disappointed in the state of her beloved hilltop.

In a moment, an entire story unfolded in my mind: a children's story, as if someone read it to me. The two worlds collided as the story filled my brain, but the commitment of a pending appointment squeezed between the lines. *I can't be late for my massage.*

My back beckoned: my commitment to personal care. "I'll return," I said to the angel, bowing. "I'm sorry about your hilltop."

Right foot, left foot, watch out for the harebells. I power-walked down the hill. *'You'll see,' said Anna. "She's real. And she's real big too.'* I recited the story over and over in my head, afraid to lose it.

I sped to my appointment and hopped onto the massage table, still running lines in my head like a theatre actor. I considered asking for a pen and paper so I could get the story out of my head and onto the page. I can safely say that I wasted that massage appointment.

Once home, I scrawled the story onto paper at the kitchen table. *'Anna began to cry. "Why would someone destroy such a wonderful place?" Anna sobbed. "Can't they see the magic?" She picked up her rock and walked along the dirt trail, looking for harebells through her tears.'*

I could almost see my sacred place in the distance from my kitchen window. I felt the presence of the earth angel. I finished the full draft in twenty minutes then closed my journal and put it away.

MANY ON THE *path*
 come and go then come again
 Each with a story

35

CHOKING THE LIFE OUT OF ME

"It's a noose around my neck," I said.

Lisa was taken aback, "Can you find a rephrase for that rather negative statement. Something positive?" We were discussing my progress with the book during a coaching call. After our call I thought about her reaction and my description. I thought deeply about it. I rephrased it for her as she seemed to need that, yet I was clear about my reference. There was an aching that accompanied the writing of the book, the completion of the story.

I would not be free until I finished the book yet completing it met with great resistance. The doubt, the fear, the anxiety, none of it was a match for the incessant pull of the book. No affliction was strong enough to loosen the grip of the noose. The noose was a safety net to ensure I wouldn't succumb to affliction. Yet releasing the noose – completing the book — opened me up to the potential for the greatest afflictions: vulnerability, exposure, and judgment. Even *that* was not strong enough to overcome the pull to write the story.

Some days I convinced myself to just drop it, the whole

thing, and then I'd feel free. I recognized how my attachment to the book caused suffering so I would decide to let it all go. For a while I would feel free of the burden, freedom from my past and the need to revisit it. Not for long though, as the noose would tighten further until I couldn't feel release unless my fingers began to click away at the keyboard, sending bits of my journey onto the screen.

Impatience also began to flow. I felt anxious to get caught up. I needed to get my past onto the page so I could live in the present. I needed to catch up to now, which felt impossible. As long as I kept writing I felt I would always be in the past. I wanted it to all be down on paper, tied up in a nice neat bow, so I could be fully in my life.

The noose appeared to be tied to a weight and I walked around every day with the noose around my neck and the weight in my own hands. I couldn't set it down. If I put it on the ground and walked away, the distance tightened the rope until I once again retrieved my weight and carried it forward with me.

No matter how many times I tried to drop it, it pulled me back. If I wanted freedom, it was in my own hands and I had to complete the book in order to drop both weight and noose to the ground. I struggled with Lisa's course, trying to make my story fluid. The daunting task of writing 70,000 words tightened the rope. I decided to enlist the help of a client and friend. I needed fresh eyes and an honest assessment of my writing.

I forwarded the first section to one of the ladies in my weekly meditation group. She had a sharp eye for detail, a gift of organization, a calm, no-nonsense business head, and she was my main demographic: a mom interested in family/life balance and a more fulfilling spiritual life. While she formulated a critique for me, we crossed paths at the school, picking up our children. We stood at the swings, each pushing a child.

"I enjoyed the story but..." she turned to face me. "I wish it was more like your stories on *Cowbird*. I liked how each short piece offered one issue to tackle, with insights and wisdom in a small bite."

I stared blankly at her. "That's the way I enjoy writing best," I said. "This continuous format is brutal. It makes my head hurt thinking about where the story is going." It was true I enjoyed writing the *Cowbird* stories more than my manuscript. They felt simple, with a completion to each one. I walked home, contemplating her words. *Why not write the way that feels natural to me?*

I sat down to write the next day, chose one particular event and brought it to completion in my hour of writing. I stopped looking toward some distant finish line and started showing up each day as I had during my year in yoga and my meditation practice since. Daily practice. I felt a renewed passion for the book and reconnected with my creative rhythm.

My muse had delivered the money; I had to deliver the goods. Spurred on by my new format, I completed Lisa's course and the first full draft of *An Accidental Awakening: It's not about yoga; It's about family.*

I celebrated with myself. I was proud of the work I'd done and the commitment to my investment. Writing gave me the greatest growth, perspective, healing and gratitude for my journey. The gift of walking back through one of the most transformative years of my life, knowing that recording those details would make the practices available to others, gave me a sense of accomplishment and the opportunity to be of benefit. To relive the experiences of that year: my first four-directions ceremony, hula-hooping in a horse-pasture, walking on hot coals, connecting with my children and reconnecting with my husband, diving deep down the rabbit hole with my dearest friend, made the writing worth the work. As Anais Nin once offered, I got to taste life twice. Bitter-sweet but satisfying.

I SHOW you yourself
  You may not always like me
  I AM your teacher

36

LEAVE OF ABSENCE

I pulled my chin above the bar. It felt good to retrace the movements my body had perfected over fifteen years - until my lower spine blew out in 2003, and at age thirty-one, life as I'd known it ended. That injury left me bedridden for thirty-three days, unable to walk, and was the catalyst to *An Accidental Awakening*.

The kids had started parkour at the local YMCA. I'd been careful when returning to the gym. No compression exercises. I enjoyed a streamlined routine that fed my great love of strength training and moving my body in exciting ways. While they learned to tumble and tuck and roll, I filled up my strength training bucket. It was only once per week and I felt confident my body could handle it.

My chin neared the bar on the next rep. I exhaled, digging deeper to clear the bar on one last exertion. Fire consumed my back. Sweat suddenly poured from every inch of my skin. Not the sweat of a good workout. Heat flushed my body.

NO! I knew this heat. Only once before. The day Steve had helped me from bed to make the painful trip to the washroom during the worst of my low back injury. Before kids. Before marriage. Before the full extent of my changing life had been realized.

I had passed out in his arms on the way to the bathroom that day. A sudden shot of electricity, I'd lost my breath and he had to lay me on the floor next to the bed. He said my eyes had remained open, but I was unresponsive. It was a scary ordeal for him. When I came-to minutes later, I remember the fire in my body. An inferno. But just that once.

And there I was again. Muscles warm from my workout, I had no loss of movement, but I knew the damage was done. I prayed my recovery would be swift. Right after I gave myself shit for returning to the gym and not just leaving well enough alone.

MY HEAD BLEW up the next day: both with pain and words as I continued to chastise myself. *You were good. Good enough. Why did you have to push it? Fuck!*

The x-ray led to an MRI, while sleepless nights piled up. My body buzzed. Electric shocks shot through my legs into my feet. My head hurt. So much pressure.

It took depression less than a week to set up camp. It was an odd darkness, not one that came from lack of sleep or pain. It seemed a foreigner who fed off the inflammation ravaging my cervical spine. My world went dark.

"I've worn this outfit every day this week," I said to Tanya as we sat on the park bench waiting for our kids to get out of school. "One thing. That's all I have the energy for. One thing per day. Apparently putting these clothes back on is it." I sat looking forward while she sat to my right. Turning my head was out of the question.

It took everything I had in me to pick the kids up from school. On the weekends I managed to shower. I didn't sleep. There was no such thing. It hurt to put my head on the pillow. My mind and body buzzed all night.

There was nothing there. All of my years of practice: the exquisite visions and colourful auras, the gift dreams and divine connection – nothing. No thing. Just blackness.

I begged the angels to come. I cried out for release. Something was broken. The bridge between Spirit and I no longer stood. I lay in the darkness. That cold emptiness. No one was coming to save me.

Pain ruled my days. Confusion, anger and aloneness ruled my nights. I spent weeks on the couch, watching afternoon movies and drinking tea. I meditated, a little. It hurt to sit upright. I couldn't drop into the space, the spaciousness. It no longer existed.

The MRI showed all the same damage I had endured in my lumbar spine thirteen years earlier, with the added bonus of bone spurs, all now in my cervical spine. Tiny discs in distress. Big impact on body and mind.

What if it never gets better? What if this is it for you? After months on the couch, waiting for the pain to subside, which it did ever so slightly, thoughts bubbled up in my brain. *If you're going to be in pain anyway, not sleep anyway, you might as well go about doing what you want to do.* There were only so many hours a person could watch Women's Network movies before it was time to get back to life.

The bridge through the sacred portal of my cervical

spine may have been broken, but I had years'-worth of visions, insight, magical experiences, gift dreams, great teachers and cosmic creativity captured in my journals. I may no longer have been able to taste the divine buffet, but I knew that it existed. I could revisit it through my writing and re-member it for others. My memories had to sustain me. Through the darkest of nights, they were often all I had to hold onto.

DARK NIGHT of the soul
Do not cling to anything
One breath at a time

37

THE AGREEMENTS WE MAKE

I scrolled through the classes on the AWCS (Alexandra Writers' Centre Society) website. Elbow on my desk, I used my palm to support my chin while I contemplated the available courses. Creative Writing Basics. *Nope*. Introduction to the Short Story. *Nope*. Mastering the Romance Novel. *Nope, though interesting*. Alberta Skies: Metaphor and Similes through Paint, Print, Prose and Poetry. *Yes!*

Poetry and painting. The thought of it lit me up. My enthusiasm grew as I read the description: "The course will culminate with a collective publishing of participants' art and writing, a book launch and talk, and a gallery exhibition of the work." *I'd be published. Then I could get over this terrifying hurdle of putting my work out there*. My enthusiasm waned as I scrolled to the fee. I'd invested dearly in Lisa's course and although I recognized it as an investment in me, I couldn't justify any more money funneled into writing. I would need to offer more classes of my own — meditation or yoga — in order to further my creative pursuits. Art and poetry would have to wait. I spent the spring teaching classes in my home studio.

Every week, I revisited the website to check enrolment. 6 spaces remaining. 4 spaces remaining. I let the spark of possibility dance inside me even though I knew it was out of reach. For the moment, the adept footsteps of the potential left marks of hope across my heart.

STEVE PACKED his things and joined his brother and sister for the long drive to the funeral two provinces over. His aunt had passed away. We'd lost Baba, his grandmother, three years earlier. She was 101. The reason to gather in Manitoba for family events disappeared with his aunt's passing. No more summers spent hiding inside from the giant Manitoba moths and mosquitos.

Steve and his family cleared out the old mobile home and helped get her estate in order. She had lived simply. An old car. An air conditioning unit wedged into the window, used sparingly during humid Manitoba summers. Bacon grease poured into a bucket under the kitchen sink. She loved her cat. He ruled the roost. You'd never know she'd won the lottery. Twice. The Western Express in the '70s (a one-hundred-thousand-dollar jackpot), and Lotto 649 (one million dollars) just years before she died. In a town of fourteen hundred people, she'd struck gold twice. But not with her health.

"Your aunt needs to buy herself some health care," I'd tell Steve. She was old school. Tough as nails. Independent. Enduring. And she left us, along with many other family members, a gift.

"What do you want to do with the money?" asked Steve.

I placed him on speaker phone while I drove the back-country roads with the kids to visit my sister. For a moment, I felt freedom. My mind raced to hiring an editor for *An Accidental Awakening*. My heart spoke up: art and poetry, art and poetry.

With the money Steve's aunt had gifted us, we each splurged a little on personal items: his, most likely golf, and mine, the art and poetry course. We invested the rest in a new vehicle (well, new to us) and retired the old Jeep that had served us well for over 13 years. It felt like Christmas. Having no children of her own, Steve's aunt may or may not have known how she played a powerful part in my creative dream. I sent her waves upon waves of gratitude and knew she was finally pain-free.

WE MAKE agreements
before we come to this place
bound to each other

38

A LITTLE MORE MY PACE

What happened next was a whirlwind. I sat around the table in the art studio loft above our teacher's garage. Introductions and sharing ensued.

"Hi, I'm Stephanie," I said while removing my sweater. "I've been writing a memoir for a couple years. I'm not sure of my next steps but it was satisfying to finally complete it earlier this year. I used to write poetry as a kid. My art skills are sorely lacking but I look forward to spending these next weeks with all of you." I had become a master at hiding my pain, and layering my clothes to accommodate the hot flashes.

"You should attend our IPAC meeting this month," our art instructor jumped in.

"A what?"

"IPAC," she repeated. "The Independent Publishers' Association of Canada. We meet once a month at the Danish-Canadian Club for a breakfast meeting. We have guest speakers from the publishing industry. You'd meet a lot of people who could help you with your next step."

"Thank you," I replied. "I appreciate that."

I ATTENDED THAT NEXT MEETING, glutenous feast and all, where John, president of IPAC, gave the opening talk. He mentioned that he was both an editor and a coach. After hearing stories from authors on the success of their books, along with writers still plodding along the path to publishing, I got up the courage to approach John. "Do you have the time and interest to read over a children's story I wrote?"

"Yes, of course," he replied in a slight British accent. "I'd like that. Please send it to me at this email address."

The moment I returned home, I forwarded John *Anna and the Earth Angel*. My note: "I'd love your thoughts on this sweet children's story. Let me know if you feel it's worth pursuing."

John became my editor and book coach.

SHIT, I'm late. What else is new? In typical Stephanie-style, I was late for my art class. *I need to bring a picture of a sky for class.* I surfed the net at lightning speed. One lesson my pain had taught me was to let go of what wasn't important or those things that required too much energy. *This will do. I can choose something better later.*

In class, we painted our select images. "You will use this image as your work for the duration of our course. You will paint it using different techniques and refine a piece of writing about it over the coming weeks," instructed our art teacher.

Shit. I'm stuck with this image. The cloud looks like a fucking pig. Great.

The weeks unfolded between art and writing classes, and Zoom calls with John on the progress of *Anna and the Earth Angel's* revisions and publishing steps. I learned to paint, stencil, stamp, and write story, Tanka and Haiku. I was still stuck with a cloud pig. And then it hit me. The first deck of divination cards I had received years earlier, even before my year in yoga, was a gift from my dear friend Anna. She'd brought them back for me from her first trip to Sedona. The Zen Koan Card Pack. Though I hadn't viewed them in years, one particular Koan popped into my mind. It's last line: *MU!* The energy of my painting came alive in Koan, whose last line emerged: PIG!

The pace of life had picked up, along with my spirits through art and writing. I spent hours Googling self-publishing steps and case stories. I made attempts at illustrating *Anna and the Earth Angel* using my newbie watercolour skills. All appeared well, but something was missing.

LEARNING IS GROWING
You must pause regularly
Listen still deeper

39

INTRODUCTION TO JOY

"I am joy." I summoned the self-imposed mantra. I sat on my front step in morning meditation, a practice I'd observed for nearly ten years. Joy was not a feeling I claimed to know much of.

"I am joy." I ran the affirmation through my body. My shoulders shirked it off. Nope. Not joy.

I must have been recently reading or listening to a teaching on joy. Be joyful. "I am joyful." The mantra hit the brick wall of my disbelief. I had no idea what joy felt like, especially with the severed connection to Spirit since my neck injury. I certainly couldn't conjure it. "I am joy." I tried again. My tummy tensed.

So I did the only prudent thing: I committed to inviting the foreign feeling into my life through my practice, but it wasn't going to work if my body kept rejecting it. Perhaps a softer approach. "I am a vessel for joy." I waited. No response. No joy came but at least my body approved of this particular reframe.

It was settled. I recited my morning mantra for over a

month while I worked with John on the editing of *Anna and the Earth Angel*, determined to invite joy into my life.

I STOOD in the doorway of the basement spare room. We used it as a space to watch movies in the evening after the kids went to bed: far enough removed from their bedrooms so as not to wake them. Christmas was only weeks away. The kids were not toddlers anymore: no need to tiptoe around bedtime and worrying if evening movies would stir them from sleep. I stood, considering the room as a spare bedroom for my parents to enjoy during their annual Christmas visit.

Within the week, we had sold the awkwardly heavy red hide-a-bed and moved the television upstairs. I taped off the baseboards and window frames with green painters' tape and was ready to give the room a fresh face.

I overestimated my abilities and painting dragged on into day two, along with intensified pain. Too late. I was committed to the task. I rubbed essential oils into my neck and popped homeopathic anti-inflammatories. The bed arrived and the kids happily set it up in the main area of the basement – my yoga/writing studio – while I raced to ready the room before my folks arrived.

"I have a Christmas present for you," I said as they came through the front door. I carried Mom's bag downstairs. "Ta-da!" I opened the door to reveal their new room, complete with artwork, new paint, curtains, and a proper bed.

"Well isn't this nice!" exclaimed Mom.

I paraded about the room using Vanna White hands to showcase the details.

"What's this your mother tells me about you writing a

children's book?" asked Dad as he set his suitcase in the room.

"Yes, I've decided to publish one of the short stories I've written."

"Well, I know this lady," he continued, "she's quite the artist. I know her husband. They were in the store the other day and she showed me some of her drawings. They're really good. The details she got in the one of a dog…"

"That's cool, Dad." His comments seemed random. "I've been painting some of my own. I'm not sure exactly what it's going to look like yet. I think I've got this."

I continued my front step meditation through the holidays. Christmas was lovely as always: mainly about the kids but that's the fun of the season, really. Mom and Dad headed home. I laundered the spare room linens and returned the room to its showroom state while I returned to *Anna and the Earth Angel* illustrations: another watercolour painting of children without faces. My art teacher told me everyone is an artist. *Clearly not everyone can paint faces.*

The phone distracted me, giving my painting time to dry while I talked to Mom.

"Hi. Your dad is wondering if you want the phone number for the artist he told you about. You know, to help illustrate your book."

"Oh! Um … I wasn't really, I mean I'm not that far along to … okay," I said, "I'll give her a call. What's her name?"

"Her name is Joy."

You made the request
    remembered what we told you
    asked for what you need

40

MOMENTOUS MYSTERY

"Is there a second book?" John asked during our bi-weekly Zoom call.

"No, I don't work that way," I replied. "Stories come to me. I don't plan them."

"Hmmm," he smiled. "A second book may change the details of the first book. I challenge you to consider a second book and write it before you publish the first."

Great. That's almost as bad as one of Leo's readings. How am I going to write a second book? That's not my process.

My mind chewed on it for a week. Hard. There was no way I was going to simply come up with a second book. Not usually one to turn down a challenge, I finally surrendered. I dropped the idea.

And then it hit me. All at once it flooded my mind. Not a new story. Not a made-up story. Another of the coulee's stories made its way to the front of the line of my thoughts. The old tree.

In the first years after moving to our community, we often took the kids on an adventure in the coulee. We pulled both of them along the walking path in the little red wagon, sippy cups and gluten-free snickerdoodles in hand. We would veer off-path at the top of the hill overlooking the city of Calgary in the distance. We'd abandon the wagon in the tree line and drop down into the coulee along the dirt path. At the bottom stood an old tree. No longer sprouting life, this tree was surely a magnificent guardian in his prime. The stripped bark revealed smooth contours. A sturdy branch reached out across the modest creek. Someone had attached a rope with a generous knot at the end.

Michael swung across the water like a great explorer, dropping onto the opposite bank. Steve held Khali in place in the air as she gripped the rope in delight. He swayed her back and forth before letting her down on the other side.

There were no bike paths then. No fat-tires carving treads through the coulee floor. There were few others we'd encounter on our walks in those early days.

There was the great tree and his rope swing. The creek and the hillside that hid us from anyone's view. Sacred coulee.

Then the overpass came. More construction. Not in the coulee of course, but changes were made. Off-ramps and bike tunnels required more space. The creek was forced to jamble around an unnatural blanket of rocks, poured into its bed in what I'm sure the city considered a functional fashion. But no one asked the creek. They took the old tree. Cut to a stump. His smaller neighbours, living and not, removed with him. I cried that day. And the day when I returned to place offerings at his feet.

I rarely enter through that end of the coulee anymore. The creek pulls itself through the tangle of rocks. Graffiti fills the retainer walls and bike tunnels. How can they not see the magic?

Perhaps I'll return and offer blessings until healing

happens: for either the creek or Stephanie. But at that moment of memory, I knew I could tell the story. That would be the second book. It offered itself to me as *Anna and the Christmas Tree*. Wrapped in the season, I was poised to potentiate magic.

WHAT PULLS at your heart
   compels you to continue?
   Write what you most feel

41

A STRAND IN THE WEB OF LIFE

I wrote *Anna and the Christmas Tree* within a day. The more I wrote, the better my neck felt. Either writing kept my mind off my pain, or moving energy through my throat chakra opened the channel. I sat at my computer, stuck on the ending. *I know it will be a bird... endangered species. I will have to figure that out later. I'll have to find an endangered bird in the coulee. It'll take research. What are the odds there's an endangered bird that lives in the coulee?*

The phone rang. "Hey, how are you? Did you guys have a good Christmas?" I asked my good friend Tanya.

"It was great," she replied. "How about you guys?" We exchanged the basic details about holiday overeating, too much sugar, far too much electronics time for the kids, and the super sub-zero temps that kept us cooped up indoors. "That's what I'm calling about," she continued. "Do you want to get the kids outside?"

"This chinook jumped the temperature from minus twenty-eight to plus two, but the wind is brutal," I said. "What if we dropped down into the coulee?"

"Perfect. That should keep us out of the wind, and off

electronics. See you in an hour?"

From the floor of the coulee, we were warm and toasty. We were also wearing our fuzzy pants. Tanya had bought a pair one year and commented how warm they were, so I picked up a pair of my own. We pulled them on overtop our regular clothes. Our happy pants.

"I have no idea what bird it will be, but I know it will be an endangered bird." I told Tanya about the new story and its ending while the kids ran along the frozen creek, full of energy and Christmas chocolates. Once dropped deep into the coulee, time held no bearing on us. The tree-bending chinook winds were imperceptible as we treaded the belly of the coulee.

The four kids ran ahead, sliding on the ice. I dawdled, snapping a pic or two here and there with my phone camera: red rosehips against hoar frost branches. Tanya wandered ahead.

"You are not going to believe this," she beamed.

I knew that smile: equal parts *of course* and *no way*. I caught up to where Tanya stood. Of all the incredible visions I'd experienced in the coulee, this one took the cake because Tanya saw it too. Anyone could see it.

Forty-feet deep into the coulee, surrounded by snow, melting hoar frost and balsam poplars, stood one lone white spruce... draped with Christmas balls.

Who decorated this? Awe and gratitude circulated under my skin. It was one thing to see a vision in my mind's eye, but to touch it, manifested in the world around me... I was lost for words. In all the years I'd walked the coulee, this was the first I'd seen a Christmas tree.

As I pulled out my camera to document the incredible event, Tanya walked to the other side of the tree. "It gets better," she sang. I joined her. Amidst all the ornamental balls was one unique decoration: a single bird. "Your book is magical," she said.

I could barely respond, nor could I put two thoughts together. I often ask to be shown the next step along my path, or at least if I'm moving in the right direction. I could not have received a more vivid, affirming and benevolent sign. *Anna and the Christmas Tree* had been written through me, or I through it: life and story merged in that moment. I wasn't sure which one I lived and which lived me.

OVER THE FOLLOWING FEW MONTHS, I completed *Anna and the Earth Angel* and prepared it for publishing. Launch date: Earth Day. I sent the files to my printer. Nothing more to do for the book. *There is one more thing.*

I slipped into my shoes and out the front door: destination earth angel. It was time to tell her of the pending book. I couldn't clean up her hilltop, but I could tell her story.

My heart grew warm as I climbed the hill, feeling her presence. Crocuses peeked through matted grass. This was the perfect time to release the book and prompt children and adults alike to follow Anna's trail. I reached the hilltop.

Before I could acknowledge the earth angel, my attention landed on a new feature among the once tall grasses, harebells and brown-eyed Susans. An orange fence covered part of the hilltop: the kind of fence we knew on the farm as a snow fence, used to keep drifting to one side. But the purpose of this fence was not to redirect snow. It wasn't a fence of construction or pending destruction. It was a fence of reclamation. The city or the community, someone, had restored the hilltop and fenced off the delicate parts. The carved trails were no more. Holes had been filled with dirt and the land's skin was smooth again. It would take time for the flora to return.

> '"That's alright," replied the earth angel.
>   "Nature will take care of that for you, if
>   you leave her to her work."... In spring,
>   crocuses, new grasses, harebells and
>   brown-eyed Susans shot up through the
>   soil. The butterflies and ladybugs
>   returned, and so did Anna.'

> — *Anna and the Earth Angel*

When Sophie had told me that day years earlier on her treatment table that I'd write children's books, I thought she'd erred. Writing children's books was never on my radar. I didn't see what she saw. And I'm glad I didn't see it. If I'd known my purpose that day, my ego would have jumped all over it, trying to make it happen on *my* timeline. Or I'd have frozen from fear, overthinking the task. I'm glad I didn't see what Sophie saw that day, otherwise, I may have missed the grand adventure that Nature unfolded before me: the mountains of California and the red rocks of Sedona, the wisdom of Hawaii and the power of plants, the bliss of Buddha and the blackness of the dark night of the soul, my sacred place and my wild sanctuary. All of it etched across my inner landscape like Paulo Coelho's *The Alchemist*: my own Personal Legend.

Embrace the unknown
     with both hands and open heart
     Invite destiny

EPILOGUE

Good Morning,

Our class will be working in the theatre at the Rocky Ridge YMCA for the next few days and will have a presentation to showcase on Friday. It will be based on the book "Anna and the Earth Angel," by Stephanie Hrehirchuk. We would like to invite all families to join us at 11:00 a.m. for a short performance in the BMO theatre. We hope that you can make it! Have a great day!

I WAS SO focused on writing a book to help adults navigate their spiritual awakenings, to help them balance family, self and spirituality, that I had no idea how much the land's stories (our stories), the Anna stories would be of benefit.

Post-publishing, I was invited into classrooms across our city to share the Anna stories with students. We talked about writing and where stories come from, art and creativity, sustainability and environmental stewardship, and that *everyone* has a story to tell. I loved every moment of it.

The morning I received this email, two days after my 48th birthday, I placed both hands over my heart and cheered out my window at the earth angel. "Your story is reaching people. The kids love you."

"*I* LOVE YOU. And I thank you."

> *"But it is the mystery of life that sustains me now."*
> *Prince of Tides*

IN GRATITUDE

I am blessed with family, friends, community, and teachers. I am grateful to my grandparents for the sanctuary that was life on the farm. I am grateful to my parents for moving us there.

I thank the coulee every time I walk there, for looking after my family. For providing a healthy, wondrous place to live. And for telling its story *to* me and *through* me.

I am grateful to those who continue to speak for the trees, the birds, the wild grasses and harebells, crow and bear. For those who put themselves between machinery and forest. For the water protectors and the stewards of the wild horses.

We each do what we are called to do. I pray you have the courage to answer the call when it comes. The strength to weather the storm of doubt, and the support of community on one side of you and great teachers on the other.

Every time I walk in nature, I offer this blessing... more of a request of you. Thank you for answering my call:

May all who come here love you more than I.

ABOUT THE AUTHOR

Stephanie Hrehirchuk is a writer, coach, spiritual seeker and teacher.

Her training includes Tibetan Breathing and Movement Yoga, raw nutrition, spinal reflexology, facial diagnosis, Qigong, Reiki, Ayurveda, plant medicine and sustainability.

Stephanie is the author of *An Accidental Awakening: It's not about yoga; It's about family*, *Nourish: Ayurveda-inspired 21-day Detox*, as well as the children's book series: *Anna and the Earth Angel*, *Anna and the Tree Fort*, and *Anna and the Food Forest*. Stephanie has a tree planted for every print copy sold of her Anna series.

She was a regular contributor at *Gaia*, with articles published at *Sivana East*, *Finer Minds*, *Guided Synergy*, and *Trifecta Magazine*. Stephanie specializes in women's issues. She blogs, coaches and teaches about nutrition, health, yoga, meditation, the chakra system, the world of self-directed publishing, parenting/motherhood and spiritual pursuits.

She still drops the occasional f-bomb. She still hangs out with Anna. There is never a shortage of tea or dark chocolate.

ALSO BY STEPHANIE HREHIRCHUK

An Accidental Awakening: It's not about yoga; It's about family

Nourish: Ayurveda-inspired 21-day Detox

From Exercise to Ecstasy: 10 ways to turn body-mind into body-mind-spirit

Children's Books

Anna and the Earth Angel

Anna and the Tree Fort

Anna and the Food Fort

Anna and the Christmas Tree

NOTES

27. herbal internship

1. University of Illinois Extension: Our Rose Garden
2. Sourced from DoTERRA essential oils website

29. packaging up my failure

1. https://www.youtube.com/watch?v=ZL4zsmtWpwQ

Manufactured by Amazon.ca
Bolton, ON